STONEWALL JACKSON

STONEWALL JACKSON
SAVED BY PROVIDENCE

David T. Crum

Stonewall Jackson: Saved By Providence
Copyright© 2024 by David Crum

ALL RIGHTS RESERVED. No part of this publication may be reproduced, distributed, or transmitted in any form or by any means, including photocopying, recording, or other electronic or mechanical methods, or by any information storage and retrieval system without the prior written permission of the publisher, except in the case of very brief quotations embodied in critical reviews and certain other non-commercial uses permitted by copyright law.

Produced in the Republic of South Carolina by

SHOTWELL PUBLISHING LLC
Post Office Box 2592
Columbia, So. Carolina 29202
www.ShotwellPublishing.com

Cover Design: Adapted from Engraving entitled: "Prayer in 'Stonewall' Jackson's Camp." c. 1866 (Wikimedia Commons)

ISBN: 978-1-963506-99-0

FIRST EDITION

1 2 3 4 5 6 7 8 9

Contents

Foreword ix

Introduction xiii

Chapter 1 1
Childhood

Chapter 2 17
West Point and the Mexican-American War

Chapter 3 33
VMI, Christian Growth, and Evangelism

Chapter 4 59
Marriage and Family Life

Chapter 5 83
Secession and the Beginning of the Civil War

Chapter 6 105
Stonewall's Last Years 1862–1863

Conclusion 137

Afterword 145

Endnotes 149

About the Author 165

Acknowledgments

I am forever thankful for and strongly recommend the works of biographers James I. Robertson Jr., Byron Farwell, and G. F. R. Henderson. Accordingly, I could not have written this book without the resources from the Virginia Military Institute, Anna Jackson, Roy Bird Cook, Robert Lewis Dabney, John Esten Cooke, and Thomas Jackson Arnold. All books and work provided great insight and primary resource material, making this book possible.

Thank you to my little research helpers—my dear son, Tyler, and my lovely daughter, Kayla. Thank you to my entire family and my beloved wife, Ailene, for allowing me to steal the dinner table conversations for the last several months to share the life of Stonewall Jackson.

I thank Sprinkle Publications for publishing such great works on nineteenth-century Reformed theologians. Thank you to my editors, including Margaret Grimm. Margaret challenged me to think deeper, and for this, I am most grateful. Lastly, thank you to Dr. Clyde Wilson and Shotwell Publishing for giving me my first publishing opportunity.

Abbreviations

WCF Westminster Confession of Faith

WSC Westminster Shorter Catechism

Dedication

I dedicate this book to my beautiful wife, Ailene. Thank you for being the amazing wife and mother that you are. I thank the Lord for blessing our marriage and helping us grow closer each day.

Foreword

THERE REMAINS AN ABUNDANCE of books written on Thomas "Stonewall" Jackson. From analyzing his military operations and leadership in battle to providing an overall biography of the man, plenty of valuable pieces are readily available. Several works on his Christian faith have also been published. The author proposes this question then: Why conduct additional research on Jackson? The journey and desire to research Jackson started during the author's doctoral program when he studied Christianity and warfare; more specifically, he completed his dissertation on the Southern Baptist Convention during and after World War II. One of the most prominent voices in the analysis was Rev. George W. Truett. Raised in North Carolina and living most of his life in Texas, he was a proud Southerner. Within his sermons, he frequently mentioned Stonewall Jackson and Robert E. Lee. It is safe to say that he maintained a soft spot for both Confederate generals.

However, one 1942 sermon resonated with the author. The nation was fighting in World War II, and Truett preached on the topics of patience and surrendering to the will of God. In particular, he quoted Stonewall, who remained submissive to the Lord's will when hit by friendly fire at the battle of Chancellorsville. Jackson declared, "Why, gentlemen, be quiet. Don't be bothered. If I live, it'll be for the best, and if I die, it'll be for the best. God knows and directs all things for the best for those whose trust is in Him, and my trust is in Him."[1]

Such an outlook on life and his potential death impressed the author. Some of us might be angry and blame the very men who just shot us, but Jackson humbly accepted the providence of God.

Who says this? Who genuinely surrenders all aspects of his or her life to the will of God, whether good or bad? Basic initial research intrigued the author further; Stonewall Jackson was a devoted Christian man who lived his life to glorify the Lord Jesus Christ. Simply, the author's research interests in warfare and Christianity remain to this day. Certainly, Christians should abhor war, and both Jackson and Truett did; however, warfare is a part of this fallen world in which we live and has constantly remained a tool for the Lord's providence. Warfare also serves as an apologetic tool and asset for the mission field.

In 2013, while working on a master's degree paper titled *The Confederate Army and God*, the author came across numerous Christian testimonies and accounts of revival in the Confederate Army. Jackson was a Calvinist who adhered firmly to the sovereignty of God, but he was more than a Calvinist. He was a confessional Presbyterian, and he undeniably embraced Reformed theology. These beliefs, being close to those of the author, piqued further interest, and an idea developed: Why not conduct a specific book on Jackson and his Christian journey and explicitly connect it to orthodox Presbyterian teachings from the Westminster Standards, including the Confession of Faith and Shorter Catechism, and leading voices of Jackson's day? Moreover, why not analyze his Christian worldview compared to the foundation of the faith, the inspired Word of God—the Bible itself?

The author remembers life outside of Christ and can only declare that the Lord Jesus Christ transformed him into His servant. It is the author's opinion and desire that the reader gain an appreciation for the Reformed teachings through the study of Stonewall Jackson. In a world where mankind constantly fights the flesh (sin), Jackson held on strong to his Lord and Savior and desired to glorify Him in all aspects of life, including obedience to His sovereign will. Westminster Shorter Catechism Q&A 1 summarizes well the beliefs and life of Stonewall Jackson:

Q. 1. What is the chief end of man?

Foreword

   A. Man's chief end is to glorify God, and to enjoy him forever.²

A question remains: Why concentrate on the connection to Reformed theology and the Presbyterian faith? The simple answer is that the author desires the reader to gain additional insight into the fundamental beliefs and doctrines of Reformed theology. The author strongly supports and embraces the idea of the invisible church. Most positively, the body of Christ comprises members of denominations throughout the world. The true church of Christianity is the body of Christ. The author also affirms that theology matters. Perhaps biased, the author sincerely appreciates Reformed theology, just as Jackson did. Stonewall and the author share several commonalities: Both came from non-church backgrounds, were unaware of Christianity, and became Reformed church members. The author's Christian testimony is like that of Jackson. The Presbyterian faith underlines the sovereignty—or Stonewall's favorite word, *providence*—of God. It made sense in Jackson's life to become Presbyterian as life circumstances, history, and God's providential dealings emphasize Reformed theological teachings.

While this approach to analyzing Jackson's faith is not new, what makes this book one of a kind is connecting his Christian journey to the teachings of the Reformed faith, more specifically Presbyterianism, during the nineteenth century. He embraced the idea of *sola Scriptura,* or Scripture alone, and viewed the Scriptures as the literal, infallible Word of God. The foundation of this book, therefore, compares Jackson's worldview to the Bible and Westminster Standards.

The theologians in this book are of the Old School Presbyterian persuasion, but it is important to understand that the Civil War created divisions among them. Leading confessional Presbyterian ministers and theologians of Jackson's day included Robert L. Dabney, William S. Plumer, James Henley Thornwell, Charles Hodge, and others. Being confessional Presbyterians meant that they adhered to the Westminster Standards without question. This too became Jackson's position. Did Stonewall Jackson live according to the Presbyterian standards and doctrine of his day? Despite often being labeled as a religious fanatic, Jackson fell in line with these confessional Presbyterian theologians. Jackson was not a fanatic; he was indeed a born-again believer—a regenerated soul—embracing the Lord and walking in His ways. He was not a perfect man and would be the first to tell you this, but his testimony and reliance on the Lord in all aspects of life will astonish readers.

This research concentrates on when and how Stonewall Jackson came to faith, and when redeemed by the Lord, how he maintained his relationship with Jesus. Jackson is an example for all believers today. The General loved the Lord and lived for His will. His testimony, sound biblical doctrine, beliefs, and theological positions are impressive. Stonewall Jackson serves as a Christian role model yet today.

Introduction

THE AUTHOR MAINTAINS the necessity of studying every part of Stonewall Jackson's life. Readers will gain insight into Jackson's upbringing and childhood, which played a pivotal role in his conversion to Christianity and the Reformed faith and in his testimony. Throughout the book, readers will walk with Jackson from West Point to the Mexican-American War, to his professorship at Virginia Military Institute, and to the Civil War. An entire chapter presents his family life, most notably his two marriages. Both wives, Ellie and Anna, played a monumental part in Jackson's spiritual life and journey. While readers may learn some details on military campaigns and new biographical information, promoting Jackson's military genius or stellar leadership is not the author's goal. The purpose of this book is to present the Christian life of Stonewall Jackson.

Chapter 1 covers the childhood and boyhood years of Jackson. Sadly, outside of the faith of his mother, who died when he was young, Jackson experienced limited Christian direction. In his later boyhood years, his interest in the Bible, prayer, and Christianity appeared. His boyhood years remain imperative and reasonably necessary in analyzing and understanding the life of Jackson better, while also allowing the reader of today to realize that you do not need to come from a strong Christian home to become one of the Lord's sheep. The Lord is sovereign and will call whom He will, regardless of your upbringing. We rejoice that our childhood circumstances do not dictate our salvation. Further, Jackson's dying mother, Julia, prayed earnestly for the salvation of her young children. May readers never underestimate the power of prayer, one of the most critical parts of Jackson's life.

Chapter 2 concentrates on Jackson's time spent at West Point and his service in the Mexican-American War of 1846–1848. He first experienced the horrors of warfare while serving his country in the engagement. Interestingly, this is when his Christian walk picks up steam. Is that not similar to the experience of many today? Jackson became a Christian through the prayers and evangelistic efforts of others, and of course, by the providence of God. His walk to the faith was both exciting and confusing to him. He explored several denominations and doctrines in Christianity and felt most at peace with Presbyterian and Reformed theology. Early chapters are short, almost gaining depth with each subsequent chapter. This is merely because the number of Christian resources slowly increases, often from a much wider audience, especially in the last two chapters.

Chapter 3 is extensive, providing insight into Jackson's career as a professor at the Virginia Military Institute. The analysis of Jackson's Christian faith begins primarily in Chapter 3. At VMI, Jackson appeared to live an honorable Christian life and became a role model in the faith. This particular chapter provides awareness of his sanctification in Jesus Christ. His family life comes to fruition in Chapter 4. Within his two marriages, Jackson grew spiritually. These unions undoubtedly played a role in his growth, as did his fellowship with other believers and mentorship from local pastors. Chapter 4 solidifies the reality that Jackson was a born-again believer, always relying on the Lord in times of trouble and despair. Important to note is Chapter 4 briefly addresses the Old versus New School Presbyterian controversy. Jackson and most of the theologians in this book were within the Old School label.

Chapter 5 focuses on the beginning of the Civil War while Chapter 6 continues to follow Jackson in his battle campaigns and ends with his untimely death. The final two chapters mainly discuss

INTRODUCTION

Jackson's faith and how he influenced his men, with some mention of critical military engagements. The author evaluates Jackson's positions on key Presbyterian doctrines throughout each chapter. This could be considered a study of history, church history, and historical theology. The latter two will connect to the theological analysis of Jackson's Christian positions, both in context and compared to the doctrines of the Presbyterian faith. In historical studies, the Scriptures teach that the Lord is the Author and Maker of all events, including history (Col.1:17). The author affirms that studying history explores God's will and providence (Ps. 103:19). Simply, this too was the view of Jackson.

While readers might admire Jackson for his brilliant military campaigns and unwavering leadership, the author believes that Jackson would most desire that his legacy be centered on his Christian faith and as a faithful servant of Jesus Christ. To understand Jackson's Christian testimony and the power of Jesus Christ, the author believes it is crucial to study every aspect of his life, which is conveyed fully throughout the chapters. Jackson suffered deeply throughout his thirty-nine years on earth. From death continually taking loved ones and becoming an orphan, to severe medical illnesses and ailments, Jackson experienced immeasurable pain. Readers will walk with Jackson from each step of his conversion and conclude with an astonishing take and view of his beliefs and theological convictions. Jackson was a steady student, always seeking to learn more about the Lord and how to please him. The author analyzes Jackson's Christian beliefs in his writings to his sister, aunt, nephew, and niece. This book would not be possible without first-hand accounts from those who knew him best; the work contains quotes from Anna Jackson (his second wife), R. L. Dabney, and other strong Christian influences in his life. From letters, personal accounts, and interactions, readers will see the beginning of Jackson's conversion to a steady reliance on Jesus Christ, always living for the glory and will of God.

The introduction's last area of discussion relates to the controversial and dividing topic of slavery and the Confederate Army. The author disagrees with the African slave trade. However, slavery is not the focal point of this book. Stonewall Jackson adhered to divine providence. Using his same logic and our shared beliefs, God acted in His Providence and ended slavery. If Stonewall Jackson had survived the war and seen the outcomes as well as abolishment of slavery, he would acknowledge that this was at the hands of his providential God. Plainly stated, the Lord ended slavery, and for this, we rejoice.

This book will confirm the legacy of Stonewall Jackson. It will vouch that Jackson was a believer in Christ and an example to us today. History must be viewed in context and from a Christian worldview. The Lord's will remains clear throughout each generation of mankind. The author does not condone the rape, murder, and ill-treatment of any person, including enslaved people. The Bible is clear about the treatment of all humans. This book will not attack the Confederates or take a side in the Civil War, also known as the War between the States, but will present the issue through the lens of Jackson himself. The author is a proud descendant of over nine veteran great-grandfathers—six who fought for the Union Army, two who fought for the Confederate Army, and one who died in action as a Confederate "bushwhacker." This war was a bloody conflict between brothers with various issues separating the two sides.

Finally, the Lost Cause debate in modern history has gained rampant force. This book does not touch on the issue. One opinion remains: It would be irresponsible, naïve, and inaccurate to claim that Christians did not partake on both sides of the war. Believers honorably served both sides of the conflict in the American Civil War. Considering providence, the Lord desired a united union to stand and abolish slavery. The Lord was with Stonewall Jackson in many combat operations where he was often outnumbered, yet His will was for the Union forces to win the war. Stonewall Jackson believed, and Reformed theology vehemently teaches, that the Lord's will (providence) always prevails. There is neither chance nor superior human intervention in deciding the fate of a battle, the outcome of a war, or the death of a person. This reflects the worldview of Jackson and historical Reformed teachings.

INTRODUCTION

A concluding question remains: To whom is this book directed and intended? The author desires several individuals to gain insight, appreciation, and wisdom from this work; however, it might be more enjoyable for certain groups. Christians—specifically believers who seek to marvel at the work of Jesus Christ and how He transforms unbelievers into His disciples—will enjoy the conversion story of Stonewall. Devoted Southerners and those who view Stonewall as a living legend in Virginia, Confederate, and United States history will be intrigued. Lastly, the casual reader and reader of warfare literature will enjoy this content. The author wishes that all readers will gain insight into the Bible and the work of Jesus and admire His saving power in a person like Stonewall Jackson.

The author prays that each reader will marvel at the majesty, love, sovereignty, grace, and mercy of our Lord Jesus Christ, who is the Maker and Creator of all history. It is only through Him that we have any comfort at all.

Chapter 1

CHILDHOOD

THE SCRIPTURES TEACH that a child's upbringing has an everlasting impact on his or her life, future, and faith (Prov. 22:6). Certainly, people can abandon their childhood instruction and turn to their own worldview; however, the adolescent years often help to mold a child's future. Not everyone is blessed to be born into a Christian household. "Children do not get to choose their parents" is often heard today. This holds especially true for those who experience pain in their young lives. Regardless of their beliefs or practicing faith, parents or guardians play a crucial role in the development and destiny of young children. Thomas "Stonewall" Jackson's upbringing was no different. Though he did not have a stable boyhood, prominent figures in his life, including his mother and one particular uncle, played a decisive role in his development. In Reformed theology, the covenant is at the core of the family. Through God's sovereignty, He will have a relationship with the parents and children in a bond that bears the fruit of faith in the generations to come. While Jackson's family did not exactly resemble such an idea, a seed appeared that resembled such a covenantal approach from the genuine faith of his mother, Julia.

Whether one is a Christian or an atheist, the reality is that everyone has a worldview. However, many people do not realize this. Worldviews correlate to one's perception of reality and life. Simply put, a worldview is one's belief within the world in which one lives. Children's initial worldviews usually develop from their parents' or guardians' teachings and instructions. It is no coincidence that experts study the early years of noticeable figures in history to determine from where their influences and thoughts were derived. Analyzing the boyhood years of Jackson helps us to understand the foundation of his life, morals, and ultimate purpose. The reader must realize that providentially the influence and practice of Christianity remained largely absent in Jackson's younger years. It is safe to say that the beginning period of Jackson's life was tumultuous and filled with sorrow and pain.

Nevertheless, Thomas inarguably grew into a man of strength, courage, wisdom, and understanding. These key fundamental traits remained with him throughout his life. While the influence of Christianity and Christian accounts were lacking in his boyhood and adolescent years, his mother planted a seed that played a meaningful role in his future spiritual life, and these years are pivotal to understanding the complete person of Stonewall Jackson.

BOYHOOD

Thomas Jackson, born January 21, 1824, in Clarksburg, (West) Virginia, to Jonathan and Julia Beckwith Neale Jackson, was named after his mother's father, Thomas Neale. While the reader might know the late General as "Stonewall Thomas Jonathan Jackson," he did not take the name "Jonathan" until several years following his childhood.

His father, Jonathan Jackson, served as a lawyer and had a reputation for being "careless with his finances and accrued much debt in his young life."[3] Interestingly, the Jackson family was uneasy about the prospective marriage of Jonathan and Julia. Most notable was the apparent concern for Julia's well-being.[4] The concerns were well-founded as Jonathan often sold goods to pay off debt. Robert Lewis Dabney, Presbyterian minister and Stonewall Jackson's former Chief of Staff, wrote the following of Jackson's father: "Jonathan Jackson, the General's father, is said to have been, what was unusual in his race, a man of short stature; his face ruddy, pleasing, and intelligent; his temper genial and affectionate, and susceptible of the warmest and most generous attachments. He was a man of strong, distinct understanding and held a respectable rank as a lawyer."[5] Dabney further supported the claims of financial issues surrounding Jonathan: "His patrimony was adequate to all reasonable wants; the lands which he inherited from his father are now so valuable as to confer independence on their present owners. But a temper too social and facile betrayed him into some of the prevalent dissipations of the country; incautious engagements embarrassed him with the debts of his friends; and high play assisted to swallow up his estate."[6]

While perhaps irresponsible in his fiscal management, Jonathan, by all accounts, loved his family and spent many days at the bedside of his severely ill daughter, Elizabeth, the eldest of his children. Sadly, young Thomas's father passed on March 26, 1826, when he (Stonewall) was still a young boy. His father contracted an illness (later known as typhoid fever) from the couple's daughter Elizabeth, who had died three weeks earlier.[7] Jonathan stayed beside six-year-old Elizabeth, nursing her until her death.[8] The passing of both Elizabeth and Jonathan altered the young family's lives.

Julia endured, remaining strong for the three surviving children. Death—a consequence of original sin—challenges everyone, though Julia, a Christian herself, knew the importance of this temporary life. Speculation ensued that the local Freemasons had helped to support the young family, of whom Jonathan was a founding member.[9] Dabney supported this conclusion, writing, "The Masonic Order, of which Jonathan Jackson was an officer, gave to the widow a little cottage of a single room."[10] Most telling of Julia: she was a woman of Christian character and a lady of faith. Her background appears to have been in the Wesleyan or Methodist circle.[11] Thomas's wife, Anna Jackson, later alluded to the impact of Julia on her children, "Such a mother could not but leave a deep impression upon the heart of such a son. To the latest hour of his life, he cherished her memory."[12] The Neale extended family practiced Christianity; they were known as devout in their faith. Her faith was evident in her perseverance and ability to continue through such dark days.

While suffering from the loss of her husband and eldest child, young Julia had no choice but to provide for her family. Census records show the family stayed in the area and later confirmed the household "owned twelve slaves."[13] Such an account supports the conclusion that she was not suffering in extreme poverty. Of importance is the fact that the extended Jackson family came from a reasonably comfortable financial line that is said to have likewise assisted the young widow in surviving without her husband. Julia also went to work in a school.

One of the first Jackson biographers, Roy Bird Cook, wrote: "A strange analogy runs through the history of Jacksons, particularly evident in a strong inclination to participate in public life. They have produced few writers and artists but many generals, politicians, and captains of industry."[14] The Jackson family had a deep-rooted connection to the United States, with ancestors deriving from the Scotch-Irish bloodline associated with Protestant theology, more specifically, from the original homeland of the United Kingdom.[15] Noteworthy is that Presbyterianism eventually became the teachings of Jackson. Some suggest that Julia took residence at the Jackson compound following the death of Jonathan and perhaps spent some time with his mother.

In 1830, "Julia married Captain Blake B. Woodson a lawyer."[16] By 1831, she had become a member of the "Clarksburg Presbyterian Church."[17] Soon after, the family moved to "Fayette County, (West) Virginia."[18] Here, Woodson became the town clerk. The remaining Jonathan Jackson children stayed in Fayette County with Woodson and their mother briefly. Differing accounts emerge; nevertheless, the three surviving Jackson children (including Thomas) were split up and left Julia and Captain Woodson's company. The eldest boy, "ten-year-old Warren, initially lived with Julia's brother Alfred Neale in Wood County, Ohio." "Young seven-year-old Thomas (Stonewall) and his five-year-old sister Laura appeared headed to another Neale family member before Jonathan's brother, John or 'Cummins' Jackson, stepped in and took the two kids."[19] Being around seven years old, Thomas remained devastated that his mother was sending him away. He spent day and night outside of his home sobbing in the forest. Biographer James I. Robertson Jr. wrote of the final meeting between Thomas and his mother before he left her company: "Julia Woodson sobbed uncontrollably as she hugged her small son and tried to tell him goodbye. The child fought back tears while being placed on a horse. As the party of riders started away, the hysterical mother ran to her son and held him once more. Julia Woodson never recovered from that farewell. As for Jackson, his second wife Anna observed many years later: "That parting he never forgot; nor could he speak of it in future years but with the utmost tenderness."[20]

Speculation remained that Julia suffered from depression and physical illness, and Woodson felt unworthy or financially unable to take care of the Jackson children. Anna Jackson, Thomas' second wife, confirmed such accounts: "Though Captain Woodson was always kind to the children, his slender means were inadequate to the support of a family, and necessity soon compelled the poor mother to give up her two boys."[21]

On October 7, 1831, Julia "gave birth to another son, Wirt Woodson."[22] Experiencing significant birthing difficulties, Julia grew increasingly ill and never recovered, passing away in December 1831."[23] A Jackson family servant named Uncle Robinson brought young Thomas and his sister, Laura, to their mother's bedside to say their goodbyes. Julia's faithfulness to Christ and Thomas' last exchange with his dying mother made an enduring impact on him, one that he held dear to his heart, and most notably played a decisive role in his future faith in Christ. Captain Woodson, the widower, spoke the following upon Julia's death: "No Christian on earth, no matter what evidence he might have had of a happy hereafter, could have died with more fortitude. Perfectly in her senses, calm and deliberate, she met her fate without a murmur or a struggle. The grave could claim no victory. I have known few women of equal, none of superior merit."[24]

Within a few short years, Thomas lost both of his parents. Thankfully, the Jackson clan stepped in to raise the orphan child. Biographies on Jackson explain that he lived in the Jackson compound with his sister, Laura. Older brother, Warren, appeared to reside with the Jacksons for some time. Stonewall's wife later reported that the extended family, including the family slaves, adored young Thomas. For a short time, his paternal grandmother assisted in raising both young children.

Within the family acreage were unwed aunts and uncles who allowed the children to wander the property. Eventually, several of the aunts married, and the grandmother passed. Jackson's nephew Thomas Jackson Arnold described the home environment:

> It was a happy home for the children. They were indulged in every way and to an extent well calculated to spoil them. In August 1835, death claimed the much-loved grandmother. The two maiden aunts had in the meantime married and were living in their own houses. As only the bachelor uncles, and the slaves, were left, the home for the children was broken up. Thomas, now nearly twelve years of age, was received into the household of a relative by the name of Brake, who lived a few miles from Clarksburg. His sister Laura, after some months spent with her aunts in the vicinity, was sent to reside with the family of one of her mother's brothers, who lived a few miles above Parkersburg.[25]

Often typical with orphans, Thomas longed for stability and a home. Little information is known, but Thomas did not care for the company of Uncle Brake, who was the husband of his father's sister, Polly. Anna stated that young Thomas constantly said, "Uncle Brake and I don't agree; I have quit him and shall not go back anymore."[26] Thomas cared deeply for his aunt but felt that Uncle Brake was too harsh and ill-tempered. Thomas, intentional in his decision, left the Brake home and made his way back to the Jackson compound, staying with a variety of relatives.

Older brother Warren, at some point, met up with Thomas, venturing from house to house within the extended family. On one occasion, Warren and Thomas took a long trip to Ohio; they were gone several months. Little is known of this trip, but it had the blessing of Uncle Cummins. Interestingly, most relatives respected Warren and considered him a trustworthy young man. Later in life, Jackson wrote great things about his older brother. He noted his prayer habits and Christian ideals. Obviously, Julia and her family had an impact on Warren, influencing his dependence on Christ. While on the extended journey with brother Warren, Thomas eventually returned to Uncle Cummins in the Jackson compound. Though the cause of death initially remained a significant mystery, brother Warren died of tuberculosis around 1841, some attributing the journey around the Ohio Valley as the culprit in his passing. Years later, Jackson wrote to Uncle Neale: "I have received no answer to my last communication conveying the sad news of my brother's premature death. He died in hope of a bright immortality at the right hand of his Redeemer. His last hours were spent in admonishing his friends who wept around his bed to flee from the wrath to come. As time is knowledge, I must hasten my pen forward. We have received the smiles of a bounteous Providence in a favorable spring."[27]

Notable in such an account is the reference to Warren's "Redeemer." In his later boyhood years, Thomas settled down on the Jackson acreage. This is where he stayed for the rest of his remaining teenage years. Biographer Byron Farwell, wrote, "His uncle Cummins was undoubtedly the greatest influence upon his boyhood."[28] Jackson later supported this in personal writings, noting that Cummins was the closest thing to an earthly father he ever had. Likewise, Cummins held a special place for Thomas in his heart.

Without a doubt, no person other than his mother made a more significant contribution to the upbringing of Jackson than his Uncle Cummins. In his younger years on the Jackson acreage, he ventured and played around the family compound like any other kid. His grandmother loved him dearly, and he was a genuine, loving, and caring big brother to his sister, Laura. Jackson's wife Anna reported, "Laura followed him everywhere, even in his rabbit hunts, in which he was quite an expert. After running a rabbit into a hollow log, he would place Laura at one end and himself at the other, and in this way they often caught the little creatures with their hands."[29] Laura remained close to him for most of his life.

Uncle Cummins was a tough man of great physical stature. He had a temper but was a hard worker and continued the Jackson family trait of always seeking additional wealth. Anna explained of Cummins, "He was a bachelor of middle age, and being a man of independent fortune and a kind heart, he was disposed to all in his power for Warren and Thomas. The latter it is said, was his favorite, and he could not have been treated with more kindness if he had been his own son."[30] Cummins provided a stable home and served as the father figure that Thomas needed in his life. Thomas helped on the acreage and worked daily with his uncle, who provided whatever he could to educate and raise the young boy. Cummins ensured that Thomas and his older brother (when he lived with Cummins) attended the neighborhood school. However, the education Thomas obtained did not meet the day's standards. Nevertheless, he received some form of education.

On the acreage, some of Thomas' duties included "transporting the stems of poplars and oaks from the woods to be converted into lumber."[31] Uncle Cummins owned hundreds of acres, continuously purchasing more land, and in 1833, constructed a dam on the property.[32] By 1837, locals knew the property as "Jackson's Mills."[33] The property is said to have been significantly destroyed years later during the Civil War.

Like Thomas' father, Cummins and his other bachelor uncles were fond of horse racing and had a "four-mile horse track on the property."[34] Thomas had the responsibility of caring for these horses. Further, his wife Anna later noted, "He was so well taught [riding] that he was never thrown off."[35] Cummins, so impressed with Thomas' horse riding, often made him the jockey in competitive races. One neighbor recalled, "If a horse had any winning qualities whatever in him, Tom Jackson never failed to bring them out on the truth!"[36] To sum up the person of his younger years, Anna wrote the following: "His temper as a boy was cheerful and generous, and his truthfulness was proverbial. There was an instinctive courtesy in his conduct; his sense of justice was very strong, and as long as he met with fair treatment from his associates, he was gentle and peaceable; but he was quick to resent an insult, and in a boyish combat would never yield to defeat."[37]

Unmistakably, living with Cummins impacted Thomas. While Cummins reared his nephew into the man he would become, Thomas' uncle was not a known Christian. However, he showed Thomas kindness, love, and direction. Whether one is in Christ or not, the Lord will use mankind for His own will, often producing good attributes, even from unbelievers. The Westminster Confession (16.7) explains:

> Works done by unregenerate men, although for the matter of them they may be things which God commands; and of good use both to themselves and others: yet, because they proceed not from an heart purified by faith; nor are done in a right manner, according to the Word; nor to a right end, the glory of God, they are therefore sinful, and cannot please God, or make a man meet to receive grace from God: and yet, their neglect of them is more sinful and displeasing unto God.[38]

Dabney remarked on this issue, "Cummins Jackson, though temperate and energetic, was himself utterly devoid of Christianity, of a violent and unscrupulous character of a sporting gentleman."[39] He added, "The Christianity of the region was not influential; ministers were few, and deficient in intelligence and weight, being chiefly the most uncultivated members of the Baptist communion, or of the itinerant fraternity of the Methodists."[40] Jackson biographer James I. Robertson Jr. wrote, "Greed and strapped finances were ultimately the doom of Cummins."[41] In his book on Jackson, author J. Steven Wilkins remarked that Cummins "could be unscrupulous and greedy; he was extremely contentious; he sometimes showed little regard for the law; he had little sympathy for religion and a great fondness for gambling, drinking, and horse racing."[42]

The Bible is clear that no man is righteous (Roms. 3:10-11); examining the boyhood years of Jackson supports the fall of mankind and sin itself (Genesis 3). The Westminster Shorter Catechism contemplates the seriousness and state of sin:

> Q. What is the misery of that estate whereinto man fell?
>
> A. All mankind by their fall lost communion with God, are under his wrath and curse, and so made liable to all the miseries in this life, to death itself, and to the pains of hell forever.[43]

Presbyterian Robert Alexander Webb described the fall, "His [Adam's] sin was both political and domestic in its character. By the fall, he lost his citizenship in the kingdom of God, and also his standing in the house of God."[44] Undoubtedly, per the Scriptures and because of the fall of mankind, all humans are dead in sin. Examining the life of Cummins, along with any person supports the biblical position of sinful trespasses.

So, it seems any significant Christian influence, absent from a few short years with his mother, never transpired in Jackson's younger years. Perhaps unusual for a boy his age, Thomas often sought time alone, meditating on the unknown. Biographer Roy Bird Cook wrote: "Thomas was addicted to spells of contemplation. Sitting by the side of the millrace or at the end of the dam, he would be seen deep in a book or engaged in silent meditation. From this he would turn with great zest to his chickens, a collie dog, and a few sheep. The barnyard occupants were a great delight to him, and he was very proud of his sheep."[45] Today, one can only speculate on the subject of Thomas' meditation. Did he think about his mother? Ponder life? Or perhaps contemplate the existence of God Himself?

Strong indications remain that Jackson felt internally that God was with him, though he was not completely familiar with the Bible and the faith. The Westminster Confession (2.1) is clear on the one true God:

There is but one only, living, and true God, who is infinite in being and perfection, a most pure spirit, invisible, without body, parts, or passions; immutable, immense, eternal, incomprehensible, almighty, most wise, most holy, most free, most absolute; working all things according to the counsel of his own immutable and most righteous will, for his own glory; most loving, gracious, merciful, long-suffering, abundant in goodness and truth, forgiving iniquity, transgression, and sin; the rewarder of them that diligently seek him; and withal, most just, and terrible in his judgments, hating all sin, and who will by no means clear the guilty.[46]

While only Thomas and God knew what thoughts the young man was conceiving in his mind, there remains a significant possibility Thomas meditated on the very existence of God and his role in the Lord's plan.

Sadly, the Jackson clan had many reputations, and being of a religious character was not one of them. Like their father, the living Jackson brothers (uncles) sought "wealth and power," as clearly seen in their love of horse racing. Dabney recounted, "Most of the men of position were openly neglectful of Christianity, and some were infidels. No one will wonder, then, that as young Jackson approached manhood, his conduct became somewhat irregular."[47] The region lacked Christian influence; few churches were in the area, and of the ones that existed, most were of only one faith: the Baptist tradition. Dabney wrote of the Jackson family, "Minds such as theirs, self-educated by the activity and competition of their bustling times, were too vigorous to acknowledge the intellectual sway of a class of ministers who dispensed, for sermons, their crude notions of experimental piety, in barbarous English."[48]

Within the area, genuine disciples were in small numbers. Perhaps similar to today, the concept of nominal Christianity, or "in-name-only" individuals, dictated the area. However, a seed of faith was in Thomas' heart—inarguably planted by Julia, and more certainly placed by the grace of God. Perhaps not knowing it yet, Jackson's future was bright and found in the light of Christ. Dabney commented, "The nephew [Stonewall] appears to have imbibed all the good traits of the uncle, and to have escaped the bad."[49] Adding further, "Was it not due to that noble constitution of his nature, that reverence for the true and the right, that manly courage which the Creator impressed upon it, for his own ulterior ends, coupled with the purifying force of a Christian mother's teachings and prayers?"[50] Christian biographer Rev. John R. Richardson agreed, "There was nothing in Thomas Jackson's early environment designed to make him a Christian. His uncle, Cummins Jackson, was energetic but was far from being a Christian. The general morals of the community were loose and irregular."[51] The reader will rejoice in the salvation found in Christ, that the most unexpected convert becomes a devout follower of the Lord Himself.

Of course, the author cannot declare precisely when the Lord softened Jackson's heart, though testimonies point to a growing interest in the faith developing in his later boyhood years. The young Jackson lived a predominately moral life, supporting the Bible's teachings of the law on everyone's heart: "For when the Gentiles, which have not the law, do by nature the things contained in the law, these, having not the law, are a law unto themselves: Which shew the work of the law written in their hearts, their conscience also bearing witness, and their thoughts the means while accusing or else excusing one another" (Rom. 2:14–15). On God's law present in all creation, The Westminster Confession (4.2) plainly states:

> After God had made all other creatures, he created man, male and female, with reasonable and immortal souls, endued with knowledge, righteousness, and true holiness, after his own image; having the law of God written in their hearts, and power to fulfill it: and yet under a possibility of transgressing, being left to the liberty of their own will, which was subject unto change. Beside this law written in their hearts, they received a command, not to eat of the tree of the

knowledge of good and evil; which while they kept, they were happy in their communion with God, and had dominion over the creatures."[52]

A later account reported that young Thomas did, on occasion, attend church services on his own. One town girl stated, "Thomas Jackson, a shy, unobtrusive boy, sat with unabated interest in a long sermon, having walked three miles in order to attend."[53] Robertson Jr. supported the evidence of spiritual interest in Jackson's life, "At an impressionable period of Jackson's life, religion entered his soul. He took it seriously. Sometime before 1841, he began praying nightly."[54] Jackson's nephew, Thomas Arnold, wrote on early religious influence and Thomas, "His Grandmother Jackson and her father's family, the Haddens, were devout Christians."[55] He added, "Many of Thomas' relatives living within visiting distance of where his boyhood days were passed, and with whom he no doubt frequently associated were pious people, so that had he grown up to be other than a man of rectitude, it would have been surprising. In letter after letter written by General Jackson in later life he refers to the blessing that should come to his sister and himself from his mother's and brother's prayers, showing that from infancy his mind was directed towards God."[56]

However, being raised primarily by the Jackson family, who did not embrace Christian teachings (Cummins), it is remarkable that Thomas maintained interest and faith in Christ. The reader can credit only God's love, grace, and sovereignty that faith developed and endured in the young man. This is evidence of the seed of faith, and the answers to the prayers of Julia.

Before obtaining a formal military education at West Point, Thomas was a deputy constable, collecting debt. He gained this position around the age of sixteen or seventeen, which was unusual. However, the local town's officials knew of his reputation, honor, and strong moral character. The vocation was difficult; he often collected judgments upon locals and even extended family. He disliked this position and longed for a change, which came with his invitation to study at West Point.

Considering the tenets of Christianity, it remains essential to address slavery when studying Jackson. From his parents owning slaves to several enslaved people being under Cummins on the Jackson compound, Jackson grew up with the institution of slavery. Was this a normal part of life for the young man? Did he have any thoughts on the issue of the day? Few early accounts exist. Biographer Roy Bird Cook wrote about Jackson as a young child that he taught one slave to read and write.[57] Interestingly enough, once the slave learned how to write, he "forged a pass and entered the Underground Railroad. Uncle Cummins was more amused than upset about the incident."[58]

Of interest is another story from biographer Byron Farwell. Young Thomas and a local friend (Joe Lightburn) saw a neighbor burying his slave who had recently died. Farwell shared the story: "Riding on, the two fell into a discussion about slavery: 'Thom. seemed to be very sorry for the race and thought they should be free and have a chance.' [Jackson] said that Joe Lightburn said they should be taught to read so they could read the Bible and he thought so too. [Jackson] told him it would be better not to make known such views."[59]

The reader cannot know Jackson's definitive feelings toward slavery, but he had an excellent reputation for treating others fairly and kindly. Most importantly, compassion deriving from the Scripture existed. J. Steven Wilkins writes, "Joe Lightburn became the first of several friends who were to have a great influence on Jackson's spiritual growth. The Lightburns were devout and educated Christians and had a sizable library from which they allowed Tom to borrow liberally."[60]

Jackson was an independent spirit. He grew up fast, relying on his own character in a life with no mother or father to care for him. Thankfully, he gained some stability in his adolescent years with Cummins. Though Cummins was a man of questionable moral reputation, he seemed to take care of Thomas and passed on to him a strong work ethic and, most importantly, discipline. Yet his mother's and her extended family's Christian influence was always present with Jackson. Perhaps, though unknown to him at that point in his life, it was but the seed of the faith laid upon his soul that would slowly grow.

Conclusion

Jackson's early life was comprised of pain, sorrow, and adventure. However, he had an extended family that cared for him. Granted, most of the Jackson clan were not of the Christian faith like his mother. Nonetheless, he learned many wonderful traits from his relatives, most notably from Uncle Cummins. By the accounts of those who knew him best, Cummins did not embrace Christianity. Yet, Jackson learned hard work, discipline, and courage from his uncle. Such traits followed Jackson throughout his remaining years, including his service in the military.

Most heartfelt was the everlasting impact of Julia, Jackson's mother. Though he experienced only a few short years with her, these years were pivotal in his upbringing and later became monumental in shaping the man he would become. Julia was a woman of faith whose death could never be erased from the mind of young Jackson. The peacefulness and obedience in death to surrendering in Christ continued with Jackson until his own death. Julia's impact on her sons' lives was everlasting: a legacy that mattered. Warren, Thomas' older brother, continued to serve as a faithful example to Thomas before his death in 1841.

While most might remember Jackson as a strong military leader, it remains important to note that he was a loving, caring brother and a boy who sought justice in life's affairs. It was entirely possible that Jackson was slowly being reared in the ways of Christ, perhaps an adoption of faith or regeneration of the soul to which he was not yet awakened.

Chapter 2

❖

West Point and the Mexican-American War

THE YEARS FOLLOWING childhood often prove to be the most critical in determining a person's livelihood. In the life span of Thomas Jackson, this is when he found his calling in life. From attending the United States Military Academy at West Point to serving in the military as an officer, Jackson continued his journey of discipline, courage, and independence. Jackson became a well-known officer, gaining the respect of those around him.

While most people might remember Stonewall strictly as a Confederate General, studying his time in the US military is essential. Jackson was a proud Virginian who served his nation with honor. His education was among the elite of the US Army officers. Further, he experienced the horrors of war with service in the Mexican-American conflict. Such experiences clearly shaped his life, including developing more understanding and interest in organized religion, specifically Christianity.

During these years, Jackson often sought out theological discussions for answers to questions. Through the process of sanctification, Jackson was like any other new convert and gradually became a faithful follower of Christ. The Lord opened his heart, and his interest in religion grew exponentially. This chapter examines Jackson's military training, engagements, and his more pronounced introduction to the Christian faith.

WEST POINT 1842–1846

Knowing that Thomas desired an education and an exit from his employment as a constable, Uncle Cummins heard of an opportunity he felt he needed to share with his nephew. An open seat remained at the US Military Academy representing Jackson's district. A local blacksmith threw out the suggestion to Cummins and hinted that Jackson could benefit from such an appointment. Cummins agreed and shared the news with his nephew.[61] While Jackson eventually received a seat at the Academy, he was the second choice, as the first candidate withdrew after one day.

Acceptance into West Point was no simple undertaking. Congressional districts appointed top applicants to the Academy. This meant that the congressman of Jackson's area (Rep. Samuel Hays) needed to accept and recommend Jackson's application to the military institute. Similar to today's requirements, he needed letters of recommendation to have any legitimate chance of approval.

With the support of "town merchants, farmers, and an established attorney named Jonathan M. Bennett," Jackson received the required blessings.[62] Bennett played an incredibly decisive role, initially reluctant to recommend Jackson. Nonetheless, after grilling him for hours, he agreed to support his candidacy at West Point[63] which, well-known for its rigorous academic studies, concerned some townspeople. While Jackson had attended school for some years, his limited education compared to other young men his age remained a viable concern. Answering his objectors, he replied, "I know that I shall have the application necessary to succeed; I hope that I have the capacity; at least, I am determined to try, and I want you to help me."[64] He added, "I am very ignorant, but I can make it up by study. I know I have the energy, and I think I have the intellect."[65]

Jackson's determination paid off, and he eventually left Clarksburg for Washington, where he met Congressman Hays. There he remained for a few days, spending time alone with Hays. In June 1842, he entered West Point as a formal cadet. The reputation of a challenging learning environment held true. One classmate wrote of Jackson:

> He had a rough time in the Academy at first, for his want of previous training placed him at a great disadvantage, and it was all he could do to pass his first examination. We were studying algebra, and maybe analytical geometry, that winter, and Jackson was very low in his class standing. All lights were put out at taps, and just before the signal he would pile up his grate with anthracite coal, and lying prone before it on the floor, would work away at his lessons by the glare of the fire, which scorched his very brain, till a late hour of the night. This evident determination to succeed not only aided his own efforts directly, but impressed his instructors in his favor, and he rose steadily year by year, till we used to say: If we had to stay here another year, old Jack would be at the head of the class.[66]

The boyhood traits of dedication, determination, and resiliency paid off. Jackson studied harder than most of his classmates, never giving up. His academic disadvantage in the Academy did not hold him back; it remained no obstacle in his drive to succeed. Dabney wrote, "The acquisition of knowledge with him was slow, but what he once comprehended he never lost."[67] The Bible supports the concept of hard work, one trait Jackson undoubtedly maintained: "The hand of the diligent shall bear rule: but the slothful shall be under tribute" (Prov. 12:24).

Life in the Academy challenged each cadet, showcasing strict military discipline. Here Jackson excelled, growing in physical stature and ability.[68] His social life remained limited, having only a few confidants and never seeking outside temptations. His wife Anna wrote, "He did not remember to have spoken to a lady during the whole time he was at West Point, but he devoted himself with all of his mind and soul to his studies, giving but little time or thought to anything else."[69] Jackson did not achieve high marks in many of the required subjects taught. He did, however, score "5th in ethics."[70] Dabney concluded, "His greatest success in ethics where his grade was 5th—a correct prognostic of that transcendent ability in statesmanship and moral reasoning, which every great commander must possess."[71]

While the training institute focused more on military standards and education principles, some Christian reasoning presented itself to Stonewall. Dabney reported: "Speculatively, he was a believer; outwardly, he was observant of the decencies of religion, and his morals were pure; but the sacred impression of his mother's piety and teachings was as yet dormant. The most authentic disclosure of his moral nature at that time is a code of behavior which he compiled for himself, and carefully engrossed in a blank book under the title 'Maxims.'"[72]

The believer today affirms that moral reasoning is an apologetic tool for the very existence of God. Such logic continues to baffle any opposition to Christianity, as there remains no answer for sin and the morality each human possesses in their mind and soul. Such tenets of ethics have long existed within military and law enforcement structures. Anna noted some of the core articles embraced by the Academy:

> Endeavor to be at peace with all men. Sacrifice your life rather than your word. Endeavor to do well everything which you undertake. Never speak disrespectfully of anyone without a cause. Spare no efforts to suppress selfishness unless that effort would entail sorrow. Let your conduct towards men have some uniformity. Temperance: Eat not to dullness, drink not to elevation. Silence: Speak but what may benefit others or yourself; avoid trifling conversation. Resolve to perform what you ought; perform without fail what you resolve. Frugality: Make no expense but to do

good to others or yourself; waste nothing. Industry: Lose no time; be always employed in something useful; cut off unnecessary actions. Sincerity: Use no hurtful deceit; think innocently and justly, and if you speak, speak accordingly. Justice: Wrong no man by doing injuries or omitting the benefits that are your duty. Moderation: Avoid extremes; forebear resenting injuries as much as you think they deserve. Cleanliness: Tolerate no uncleanliness in body, clothes, or habitation. Tranquility: Be not disturbed at trifles, nor at accidents, common or unavoidable.[73]

While not exclusively resembling the teachings of Jesus, the West Point cadets unquestionably held a moral compass similar to those teachings in the Sermon on the Mount (Matthew 5-7). With such an emphasis on moral standards, without question, the cadets often speculated on the author of morality. Within a few short years, Jackson knew quite well the answer to such a thought. Some connection to Christianity existed at the Academy, as the local chapel was Episcopalian to which attendance was mandatory.

Jackson graduated after four years of strenuous studies on June 30, 1846.[74] Undoubtedly, the heavenly gifts of wisdom and instruction remained with Stonewall. He persevered until the end, graduating from the United States Military Academy and becoming appointed as an officer in the US Army. Known to the officers in training was the growing tension with Mexico. Jackson commented on this in a letter to his sister on April 23, 1846: "Rumors appear to indicate a rupture between our government & that of the Mexican. If such should be the case the probability is that I will be ordered to join the Army of occupation immediately & if so I will hardly see home until after my return & the next letter that you will receive from me may be dated Texas or Mexico."[75]

MEXICAN-AMERICAN WAR 1846–1848

By the time Jackson graduated, America was at war. The military wasted no time; Jackson, a second lieutenant, received his orders to the "First Regiment of Artillery."[76] Arriving in New Orleans, he set sail to Mexico for immediate field duty. Anna wrote, "The war continued two years, and Jackson was in most of the battles that were fought from Vera Cruz to the fall of the capital, which ended hostilities."[77] Mexico left a great impression on the young officer. Years later, he recalled that he preferred the climate and scenery to that of his homeland. Undisputedly, the war also challenged Jackson in mental and emotional fitness, as the horrors of battle confronted the soul.

To no one's surprise, Jackson flourished in command. Under contest and high-stress situations, he earned a reputation as a brilliant military commander, making quick decisions that assisted his fellow men in victorious battles. In his book on Stonewall, James Robertson Jr. wrote, "Jackson had his first encounter with War at Veracruz. His behavior was that of a veteran as he moved from gun to gun and supervised the salvoes. His behavior under fire attracted notice throughout the siege."[78] He added, "An academy classmate who watched Jackson at one point in the bombardment stated that 'Old Jack' was as 'calm in the midst of a hurricane of bullets as though he were on dress parade at West Point."[79] His reputation as a formidable military leader grew, and Jackson dominated in any high-stress combat situations. Christian biographer John Richardson wrote: "Apparently, courage was not a difficult virtue for Jackson to acquire. To a large extent he was born with it. With men falling dead all around him and fire growing hotter and hotter, he was always in perfect possession of his faculties and his mind was clear under all circumstances. It has been said that Jackson was at his best when enveloped in fire and smoke."[80]

The horrors of war did impact him. After the Battle of Cerro Gordo, he witnessed the "destruction of war seeing the dead corpses."[81] He later recalled, "this filled me with as much sickening dismay as if I had been a woman."[82] Robertson remarked, "Jackson now realized as well that he could not stand to witness suffering."[83] Further battles ensued, with the US military becoming victorious in expanding the disputed western territory. He experienced other skirmishes, as evident in the Battles of Contreras, Chapultepec, and Mexico City. With victory, the engagement called for military occupation, during which Jackson remained in the country for some time. When asked if he held battle anxieties and fears of dying he is said to have answered, "No, the only anxiety of which he was conscious in any these engagements was a fear, lest he should not meet danger enough to make his conduct under it as conspicuous as he desired; and as the fire grew hotter, he rejoiced in it as his coveted opportunity."[84] Jackson received a promotion in his rank during his service there. He also realized that his true calling in life was military service. He flourished when involved in any military engagement.

While psychological battle wounds impacted Jackson, recent accounts criticize Stonewall for his service in the Mexican-American War. Most notable from his critics is, on one occasion, his decision to ignore direct orders to retreat and continue attacks on Mexican Cavalry. Interestingly, however, Jackson received recognition for enduring the fight and did not receive any punishment from his high-ranking superiors. Another criticism centered on his unit killing civilians, including women and children. As war itself holds a reputation of being a brutal dark event that undoubtedly produces the worst traits and attributes of humanity, Stonewall's actions cannot be excluded here. There is no excuse for any intentional firing upon civilians; however, differing accounts emerge on deliberate bloodshed of civilians, as some writers note that his unit followed direct orders in their bombardment of and firing on immediate targets. Such reports typically refer to the invasion of Mexico City. On the war itself, President Ulysses S. Grant later remarked that it was one of the most unjust altercations in U. S. history.

War is not pretty; dark accounts of the horrors of battle remain throughout history. While Western powers have modernized the rules of combat, atrocities persist yet today. The Mexican-American War was no different. Dabney later remarked that Christianity helped cool the temperament of Stonewall, including his apparent love or passion for warfare. War is a reality in this fallen world, and Christians have always engaged in global conflicts. To fairly analyze Jackson and his involvement in warfare, understanding the context of the era and the situation of combat as well as the reality of sin is of utmost necessity. The Scriptures are clear that a constant battle of flesh (sin) versus Spirit remains in each believer (Gal. 5:17). Young Stonewall's soul was being drawn to Christ, if he was not already a young babe in the faith.

During Jackson's service in Mexico, his apparent Christian conversion became evident. John Esten Cooke, biographer, wrote on Stonewall's love for the War itself, "Until greatly changed by religious feeling, he seems to have loved fighting for its own sake; and it is certain that he performed his military duties in Mexico with the greatest gusto."[85] Albeit definitive conversion or testimony of the faith remains uncertain during the Mexican-American War, Stonewall frequently conversed about religion, specifically Catholicism. Moreover, the convictions and testimonies of Christian soldiers and officers in his company appear to have influenced him and his philosophical thought. Having spent significant time in Mexico, Jackson became increasingly familiar with Mexican customs and traditions, not surprisingly primarily influenced by Catholic teachings. On one occasion, he remained "confused at the sight of a young Mexican woman seen standing in front of a church statue crying."[86] In one letter to his sister, Jackson frequently referred to God: "I throw myself into the hands of an all-wise God, and hope that it may yet be for the better. It may have been one of His means of diminishing my excessive ambition; and after having accomplished His purpose, whatever it may be, He then in His infinite wisdom may gratify my desire."[87]

Compared to other letters written to his sister in previous years, these references to God are remarkable. Not only does his acknowledgments of God submit to His authority, but also seem to ascertain the need for the Lord's guidance and will. Presbyterian minister William S. Plumer (1802-1880), similarly defined the idea: "God's Providence is Supreme, and therefore sovereign. He is the sole arbiter of events and destinies."[88] He added, "It is as clear that God rules alone as that he rules at all, that he rules everywhere as that he rules anywhere; that he governs all agents, all causes, and all events, as that he governs any of them."[89] The WCF 5.1 asserts:

> God the great Creator of all things doth uphold, direct, dispose, and govern all creatures, actions, and things, from the greatest even to the least, by his most wise and holy Providence, according to his infallible foreknowledge, and the free and immutable counsel of his own will, to the praise of the glory of his wisdom, power, justice, goodness, and mercy.[90]

Another biographer, John E. Cooke, noted, "It would seem, indeed, that even at this early period of his life, he had fully embraced that doctrine of predestination which undoubtedly marked his character very strongly in latter years."[91] He continued, "He espoused the Presbyterian doctrine of Providential supervision and direction of human affairs, to the fullest extent; and had but one feeling, which may be accurately summed up and expressed in the words, 'Do your duty, and leave the rest to God.'"[92] Clearly, at this point in his life, Jackson appeared to have surrendered life's events and occurrences to the will of God. Astonishingly, Jackson realized his soul was in the hands of a Providential Creator—his Lord and Savior, Jesus Christ. Jackson's conversion and sanctification process is not surprising to the modern-day believer, as the procedure is often unexpected, confusing, and lengthy.

During the occupation of Mexico, Jackson lived among some "ecclesiastics of a nearby church."[93] Likewise, Colonel Frank Taylor became somewhat of a spiritual mentor for Jackson. Dabney rejoiced, "But we have now reached the most important era in Jackson's life; the beginning of a vital change in his religious character."[94] Jackson, convicted of his sin, knew morality was connected to the Lord. No human is without sin, and this thought-provoking concept assisted in the conversion process. Of being "dead in sin," *The Westminster Confession of Faith* asserts:

> By this sin they fell from their original righteousness and communion with God, and so became dead in sin, and wholly defiled in all the parts and faculties of soul and body. (6.2)
>
> Every sin, both original and actual, being a transgression of the righteous law of God, and contrary thereunto, doth, in its own nature, bring guilt upon the sinner, whereby he is bound over to the wrath of God, and curse of the law, and so made subject to death, with all miseries spiritual, temporal, and eternal. (6.6)[95]

Dabney continued on the impact of Colonel Taylor, "His instruction and prayers had produced so much effects as to awaken an abiding anxiety and spirit of inquiry in Jackson's mind. He acknowledged his former practical neglect of this transcendent subject and deplored the vagueness of his religious knowledge."[96] Jackson came to an understanding of his sin and realized such ways would not go unpunished. The Westminster Shorter Catechism addresses such reasoning:

> Q. What is effectual calling?
>
> A. Effectual calling is the work of God's Spirit, whereby, convincing us of our sin and misery, enlightening our minds in the knowledge of Christ, and renewing our wills, he doth persuade and enable us to embrace Jesus Christ, freely offered to us in the gospel.[97]

Anna described the impact of Taylor on Jackson: "Colonel Francis Taylor was an earnest Christian, who labored much for the spiritual welfare of his soldiers. He was the first man to speak to Jackson on the subject of personal religion, with whom the sense of duty was so strong that once convinced that a thing was right and that he ought to do it, he immediately undertook it, and so he resolved to study the Bible and seek all the light within his reach."[98]

Rev. John R. Richardson also wrote of the influence of Taylor: "Col. Taylor's instructions to and prayers for him awakened in him religious anxieties. Jackson acknowledged his neglect of this great subject of religion and deplored the inadequacy of his religious knowledge. He therefore felt that it was his duty to know more about religion and since he had always been devoted to duty, he began at once to perform it. He decided to make the Bible his study and to study all creeds and denominations with an unbiased mind."[99]

Jackson frequented meetings and fellowship with local Catholics in Mexico, including the archbishop of the region.[100] During this time, countless conversion attempts existed to bring Jackson to the Catholic faith. Dabney points out, "The inquirer Jackson departed unsatisfied, clearly convinced that the system of the Bible and that of Rome were irreconcilable and that the true religion of Jesus Christ was to be sought by him elsewhere."[101] Jackson's wife Anna wrote similarly, "His preference for a simpler form of faith and worship led him to wait until he could have the opportunity of learning more of other churches."[102] One thing remained; Jackson more openly embraced biblical teachings. The WSC references such convictions found in Scripture:

> Q. What do the Scriptures principally teach?
>
> A. The Scriptures principally teach what man is to believe concerning God, and what duty God requires of man.[103]

From the instruction of Colonel Taylor, Jackson knew the meaning of life and expectations for his own soul were found directly in the Scriptures. "Then said Jesus to those Jews which believed on him, If ye continue in my word, then are ye my disciples indeed" (John 8:31).

He forbade "all profanity within his military order."[104] Here again, a change of character and morality developed further. As he started to increase his prayer habits, Jackson often prayed for direction, understanding, and forgiveness. Such signs supported his conversion as outlined in the WCF 15.6:

> As every man is bound to make private confession of his sins to God, praying for the pardon thereof; upon which, and the forsaking of them, he shall find mercy; so, he that scandalizeth his brother, or the church of Christ, ought to be willing, by a private or public confession, and sorrow for his sin, to declare his repentance to those that are offended, who are thereupon to be reconciled to him, and in love to receive him.[105]

Like other new converts to Christianity, Jackson aspired to gain more knowledge of the faith. His intentional theological conversations with high-ranking Catholics affirmed his desire to know and learn more about Christ. Jackson had little understanding of organized religion. His mother, of a Methodist background, remained the most prominent Christian figure at any point in his life. At West Point, he became more familiar with the Episcopalian Church. Colonel Taylor, too, was a devout Episcopalian.[106] From personal accounts, Jackson read the Bible often while in Mexico and sought to obey such commands found in Scripture: "Jesus answered and said unto him, If a man love me, he will keep my words: and my Father will love him, and we will come unto him, and make our abode with him" (John 14:23).

In the summer of 1848, US troops left Mexico. Placement orders had Jackson stationed at "Fort Hamilton, Long Island for two years."[107] To his delight, Colonel Taylor lived nearby, and Jackson became more deeply involved in biblical studies and personal Bible readings. Anna wrote, "The chaplain of the garrison at that time is said to have been a Rev. Mr. Parks, to whom Major (promoted) Jackson became much attached, and at whose hands it has been reported that he received the sacrament of baptism."[108] Some family accounts had Jackson reportedly baptized in the Presbyterian church when his mother married Captain Woodson, but Jackson was never aware of this assertion, nor did he have any documentation of such an event, so he proceeded with baptism on Sunday, April 29, 1849.[109] Anna concluded on the topic:

> Although he had applied for and received the sacrament of baptism in the Episcopal Church, his mind was not yet made up on the subject of churches, and he chose to wait for further opportunities of acquainting himself with the creeds, [sic] But having accepted Jesus Christ as his Savior and Redeemer, he wished to avow his faith before men, and became a member of that Holy [c]atholic Church [the body of Christ] who creed embraced [sic] by all evangelical denominations.[110]

After his two years of duty in New York, the Army transferred Jackson to Fort Meade near Tampa, Florida.[111] Then in 1849, Uncle Cummins died. He had left Virginia for the California Gold Rush. Within six months, he succumbed to a fever. In a letter to James Jackson, another uncle, Stonewall wrote, "Though the rumor of Uncle Cummins' death may be true, yet I cannot believe it without further evidence. I shall write to California and try to ascertain."[112] The confirmation of Cummins' death was present in a letter Stonewall wrote to his sister, Laura: "Uncle had recently received a letter from our cousins in California and they say that Uncle Cummins is undoubtedly dead. This is news which goes to my heart, uncle was a father to me."[113]

By 1851, Jackson had finished his duties in Florida. He gained an appointment at the Virginia Military Institute as a professor. Excited to head back near his home, he wrote to his sister: "My Dear Sister, Good news, I have been elected Professor of 'Natural & Experimental Philosophy' in the 'Virginia Military Institute' and you may expect me home in the latter part of June. Your Bro. P.S. I am recovering from a recent attack of sickness and owing to the weakness of my eyes do not like to write myself."[114]

Jackson's achievements in battle and education paid off, as he became an instructor of aspiring cadets. Not surprisingly, the appointment in philosophy showcased his talents from the high marks he had received during his time at West Point. In just a few short years, Jackson grew up from a teenager to a combat veteran who honorably served his country. However, most impressive was his apparent outward and inward conversion to Christianity.

Conclusion

Receiving the promotion to Major Thomas J. Jackson, Stonewall became a great military leader in the US Army. The traits and discipline he learned from his education at West Point shaped the young military leader into a famous skilled commander. He had the respect of those serving under him as well as fellow officers working with him. It is no surprise that Jackson flourished under tense situations like combat. His childhood and resiliency in boyhood enabled him to endure such difficult times. Yet, it was the Lord Himself who provided safety for Jackson. On more than one occasion, Jackson escaped death clearly by God's grace. The Lord remained unfinished with Jackson and sought to develop this soldier into a true disciple.

His growing interest, studies, and faith in Jesus Christ were most impressive during his time in the war. While not part of a formal denomination during his time in Mexico, Jackson explored the faith. He studied himself and engaged in deep-rooted theological conversations. All signs pointed to conversion with his growing interest in the tenets of Christianity. This came to reality with his baptism in New York. From his letters to accounts from those who knew him, Jackson sought a personal relationship with Jesus Christ. He also surrendered to the will of God and realized he had a sovereign Creator whose divine providence would be done in his life. This resulted in a remarkable turn of events in the life of Jackson, as his Creator became a focal point in his daily affairs. One can only ponder the reality and darkness of evil experienced in warfare and perhaps attribute such encounters as the primary point of conversion in Jackson's life. This remains a plausible theory and a similar occurrence in many modern-day soldiers' lives. The harsh realities of war often shake the souls of the toughest of men.

Chapter 3

❖

VMI, Christian Growth, and Evangelism

FROM 1851 TO 1861, Jackson served as a professor at the Virginia Military Institute. During these years, he grew in his faith. He also experienced trials and tribulations that ultimately challenged his dependence on the Lord. While perhaps neither the most exciting nor prized professor, his interest in warfare remained clear. Ultimately, he passed his knowledge of war studies down to students from around the region. His firsthand experience in combat made him a unique educator.

Besides covering his professorship, this chapter will survey Jackson's faith. Life's circumstances constantly challenged Jackson's Christian worldview. Seeming to resemble his childhood years, this decade brought Jackson much pain. From losing his first wife to losing two children as a new Christian, his assurance in Christ appeared to be tested more than ever before. Noticeably, this chapter will only briefly address his family life. The subsequent chapter will exclusively cover such events.

Therefore, this chapter's theme might be best described by such terms as faithfulness and submissiveness to God's will. Stonewall grows in his walk with Christ, makes a public profession of faith, and appears to embrace a worldview centered on his Lord and Savior, Jesus Christ. For the first time in his young life, Jackson was manifesting himself as a man of prayer and obedience and submitting his will to that of the Lord. Evangelism became essential to him, especially in sharing the Word of God with his sister. Undoubtedly, a regeneration of the soul emerged.

1851–1853

In August 1851, Jackson began his professorship at the Virginia Military Institute (VMI). Although the war in Mexico had ended, Jackson felt his place was rightfully in the nation's service in the field. But with many high-ranking officials, including friends, aware of his ongoing health issues, an appointment to VMI in Lexington, Virginia, only made sense. Modern biographers often speculate if his debilitating physical condition played a role in his appointment as professor versus continued duty in the field. Speculation also continues to this day of precisely what Jackson suffered from physically, but it is credible that he experienced severe gastrointestinal issues and complications with his eyesight. In his letters to his sister, Laura, especially during the Mexican-American War, he wrote of a strict diet. At the time of his death, he had not drunk tea or coffee for over ten years, realizing the discomfort it caused to his digestive system. Stonewall experimented with what his stomach could tolerate in both beverages and food. His diet consisted of bland foods, including lemons, and water, as gastrointestinal flare-ups were a regular occurrence. Laura often inquired about his health in her written exchanges with him. Regardless, Jackson suffered frequently, and his superiors, especially those closest to him, knew this.

Becoming a professor at VMI was no straightforward task. The school itself had only a handful of instructors. His official candidacy and eventual appointment came by the pen of high-ranking officials he served with while in Mexico, including Major D. H. Hill.

At VMI, Jackson served as a professor of natural and experimental philosophy.[115] He taught such courses as physics, astronomy, acoustics, optics, and other scientific modules of study. Later acknowledged by Jackson himself, this was not his first choice.

After a few years of service at the institute, he applied for another position, professor of mathematics, but his application was not successful.

Biographer John Esten Cooke contemplated the change from military field service to the classroom and its impact on Jackson: "It must have been a hard struggle with the young soldier. The camp had now become his home: the service his chosen occupation, in which were centered all his joys and aspirations. (Thus) bending all his energies in a different direction, make usefulness his aim, no longer military glory. His health, or other circumstances, however, decided him."[116]

While his class load grew over time at VMI, initially Jackson taught "two and a half hours in the morning and conducted drill each afternoon."[117] Life at VMI was no simple task for the instructors. The cadets, who were primarily teenagers, had a reputation for being "free-spirited" and often difficult to discipline. These young men were still growing up, finding their way, and often preoccupied themselves with immature play or chasing local town girls at any opportunity. Jackson abhorred laziness and disrespect, so these cadet behaviors constantly challenged him while at VMI.

Supporting the idea of physical exhaustion as the primary culprit for VMI appointment, Anna wrote:

> At the time of Major Jackson's acceptance of this professorship, his health was not good, and his eyes, especially, were so weak that he had to exercise great caution in using them, never doing so at night. Thus crippled for his work, a friend asked him if it was not presumption in him to accept the place when he was physically incapacitated to fill it. His answer, "Not in the least. The appointment came unsought and was therefore providential: and I knew that if Providence set me a task, he would give me the power to perform

> it. So I resolved to get well, and you see I have. As to the rest, I knew that what I willed to do, I could do."[118]

Jackson believed in an active God who guided his life, including his physical capabilities and illness. In the November following his professorship, Jackson became affiliated with the Presbyterian Church in Lexington, Virginia.[119] Anna wrote, "The pastor of the Presbyterian church, Dr. William S. White, was a devout and earnest man of God, whose kindness and affability made him very winning to the young and strangers."[120] White played an essential role in Jackson's life. Presbyterians distinctively prided themselves as adherents to the teachings of some of the great Reformers, such as John Knox and John Calvin; the latter from whom the core tenets of Calvinism are most notably derived.

On November 22, 1851, Jackson made a public profession of faith.[121] The decision was not exactly straightforward; nonetheless, Jackson became a Presbyterian. Interestingly, he initially remained reluctant to embrace the fundamental principles of Calvinism and often pondered the concept of free will. "His opinions, at that time, leaned strongly to the system known as Arminianism."[122] Free will is best described by the WCF:

> Man, by his fall into a state of sin, hath wholly lost all ability of will to any spiritual good accompanying salvation: so as, a natural man, being altogether averse from that good, and dead in sin, is not able, by his own strength, to convert himself, or to prepare himself thereunto.[123] (7.3)

> When God converts a sinner, and translates him into the state of grace, he freeth him from his natural bondage under sin; and, by his grace alone, enables him freely to will and to do that which is spiritually good; yet so, as that by reason of his remaining corruption, he doth not perfectly, nor only, will that which is good, but doth also will that which is evil.[124] (9.4)

After many thought-provoking conversations and personal meetings with Rev. Dr. White, Jackson fully embraced Presbyterian understanding. He admired the theological teachings of White. Years later, he even became a deacon within his home congregation.[125] While initially confused regarding some elements of the faith, including free will and sovereignty, Jackson felt most comfortable with the Presbyterian Church. This is not entirely surprising, as past letters during the Mexican-American War attributed his wellness and safety to the will of the Most High. On the complex issue of God's Eternal Decree, the WCF teaches the following:

> As God hath appointed the elect unto glory, so hath he, by the eternal and most free purpose of his will, foreordained all the means thereunto. Wherefore, they who are elected, being fallen in Adam, are redeemed by Christ, are effectually called unto faith in Christ by his Spirit working in due season, are justified, adopted, sanctified, and kept by his power, through faith, unto salvation. Neither are any other redeemed by Christ, effectually called, justified, adopted, sanctified, and saved, but the elect only.[126] (3.6)

With its deep connection to the Protestant Reformation, Presbyterianism connected to Reformed theology. It was one of the original doctrines that separated from the Roman Catholic Church. Presbyterians played a meaningful role in the development of modern-day Europe, notably Great Britain. Further, the belief system largely influenced the Pilgrims and Puritans who established the colonies. Of the core principles were the teachings of a sovereign, active Creator. Simply, Reformed theology embraced the idea that God's hand was in history; no act was performed by free will, yet by the very hands of an active Creator. Presbyterianism focused on the "doctrines of grace," or, in simpler terms, salvation received only by the grace of God. "All Glory to God" perhaps best described their motto. The WCF 7.4 teaches the following:

> This covenant of grace is frequently set forth in Scripture by the name of a testament, in reference to the death of Jesus Christ the Testator, and to the everlasting inheritance, with all things belonging to it, therein bequeathed.[127]

The covenant of grace emphasizes the connection to salvation, found only in Jesus Christ, the Redeemer. Salvation is never earned, nor warranted, but by the grace of God, He saves His sheep. Presbyterians and members of Reformed theology, strongly adhered to Scripture alone, one of the key principles of the Protestant Reformation—sola Scriptura. They also strongly taught that Jesus remains the foundation of the faith. Theologian Charles Hodge (1797-1878) wrote:

> Christ is the great object of the Christian's faith. We believe Him, and we believe everything else on His authority. He hands us the Old Testament and tells us that it is the Word of God, that its authors believe on His testimony. His testimony to His apostles is no less explicit, although given in a different way. He promised to give them a mouth and a wisdom which their adversaries could not gainsay or resist. He told them to take no thought what they should say, "for the Holy Ghost shall teach you in the same hour what ye ought to say." (Luke 12:12)[128]

What separated adherents to Reformed theology was that God was utterly sovereign, and the Lord's will would constantly remain accomplished in all aspects of life. One core element is the election of souls: the concept that one cannot be a follower of Christ without the Lord ordaining such an event. Dabney remarked, "We believe that God's election of individuals is unconditioned and sovereign."[129] Interestingly, such teachings resembled the logic of Stonewall visibly portrayed in his letters and his thought process in years prior, specifically those during the Mexican-American War. Granted, such discussions on free will are confusing and often difficult to embrace. Nevertheless, they resembled his initial thoughts in the beginning years of his faith and introduction to Christianity. On the concept of free will correlated to salvation, the WCF 9.3 teaches the following:

> Man, by his fall into a state of sin, hath wholly lost all ability of will to any spiritual good accompanying salvation: so as, a natural man, being altogether averse from that good, and dead in sin, is not able, by his own strength, to convert himself, or to prepare himself thereunto.[130]

In reality, it was not a surprise that Jackson embraced Presbyterian theology. It almost seemed it was his destiny, as his ancestors from generations before hailed from Presbyterian-run areas in Scotland and Ireland. Being viewed as covenantal, the Lord clearly had a purpose for Jackson, and this only grew clearer as the years passed.

Dabney, a Presbyterian minister, recalled that Jackson initially struggled to include Presbyterian teachings in his understanding of Christianity. However, on his sincerity, Dabney penned, "It may be safely declared that, from the beginning, Jackson's religious character was strictly sincere, and conscientious above most Christians. This was a trait to be expected from the operation of the Holy Spirit upon a nature so decided in temper and clear in judgment as his."[131]

What is certain is that Jackson maintained a new love for God. The Lord mellowed his personality and placed in him a type of peace and understanding he had not yet experienced. Supporting this view, John Esten Cooke wrote, "He had become a professor of religion, and would have engaged in no military service but one really defensive; and while desirous of honorable regard, his great aim was duty—good to be done—an approving conscience, and the glory of God."[132] The Lord was at work in Jackson. Such growth is referred to as sanctification in the WSC:

Q. What is sanctification?

A. Sanctification is the work of God's free grace, whereby we are renewed in the whole man after the image of God, and are enabled more and more to die unto sin, and live unto righteousness.[133]

In being sanctified, the believer grows in understanding and brings forth the fruit of the Spirit (Gal. 5:22–23). Of importance, this is not of the doing or "good works" of the human, but strictly the work of the Spirit in and through the Christian.

In the classroom at VMI, Jackson faced an uphill battle. Most students did not care for him. He came across as dry, strict, and lacking patience. Biographer Byron Farwell wrote, "In classrooms, Jackson revealed himself a disaster as a teacher. He lectured in a high-pitched drawl and in a concise, didactic manner unrelieved by digressions or allusions. It was said that he never descended to the level of his pupil's understanding."[134] John Esten Cooke wrote, "It [Stonewall] was the figure of a tall, gaunt, awkward individual, wearing a gray uniform, and apparently moving by separate and distinct acts of volition."[135] He added: "In lecturing to his class, his manner was grave, earnest, full of military brevity, and destitute of all the graces of the speaker. Business-like, systematic, somewhat stern, with an air of rigid rule, as though the matter at issue was of the utmost importance, and he was entrusted with the responsibility of seeing that due attention was paid to it—he did not make very favorable impression upon the volatile youths who sat at the feet of this military Gamaliel."[136]

Cadets constantly challenged Jackson. Students often mocked him behind his back. Further, he endured complaints, including having to sit in a hearing from the board, where disciplinary action or even his potential removal from VMI was at stake. He prevailed in this case.

The classroom in Virginia was not the battlefield. During afternoon drills, however, Jackson's temperament changed drastically, often garnering the attention of the cadets. One cadet later affirmed this: "As soon as the sound of the guns would fall upon ears, a change would seem to come over Major Jackson. He would grow more erect; the grasp upon his saber would tighten; the quiet eyes would flash; the large nostrils would dilate, and the calm, grave face would glow with the proud spirit of a warrior. I have been frequently struck with this and have often called the attention of others to it."[137]

The difference clearly expounded the fact that artillery and military drills were the passion of Jackson while at VMI. Perhaps memories of his past and an adrenaline rush provided new excitement, reminding him of his time in combat. While he might have enjoyed such drills, his cadets typically did not. There were no horses to move cannons to and from; therefore, the young men tirelessly rotated the enormous weapons into position, an uphill task for any man.

Jackson longed for discipline and order, traits that Uncle Cummins passed down to him. As a man who had lost both parents in childhood and lived as an orphan, it was tough to gain sympathy from Jackson. He expected the best out of his cadets and had little patience for immature behavior and games. Jackson grew up much faster than the cadets he was to instruct. Combat experience in Mexico had contributed to his personal maturity and development.

While he struggled in his lectures and academic duties in the classroom, Jackson excelled in his walk with the Lord, constantly praying and reading Scripture. He prayed morning, day, and night. The professor would not start his day or escape the evening without prayers to his Savior. Presbyterian minister William S. Plumer acknowledged the importance of prayer: "There is no mightier influence exerted by creatures than that found in prayer. The history of human salvation is a history of the power of prayer. It is God's memorial in every generation, that he heareth prayer."[138] In the Scriptures, too, one learns the expectation of prayer: "Evening, and morning, and at noon, will I pray, and cry aloud: and he shall hear my voice" (Ps. 55:17). Hodge expanded on the teaching of prayer: "Prayer is the soul's conversation with God. Therein we manifest or express to Him our reverence and love for His divine perfection, our gratitude for all His mercies, our penitence for our sins, our hope in His forgiving love, our submission to His authority, our confidence in His care, our desires for His favour and for the providential and spiritual blessings needed for ourselves and others."[139]

Jackson's letters bring insight into his growth and views of Christianity. Interestingly, he soon embraced apologetics, perhaps underlining his past interest and achievements in the fields of ethics and philosophy. In one impressive letter to his sister in 1852, he penned:

> The best plan that I can conceive of an unbeliever in God as presented to us in the Bible, is first to consider things with reference merely to expediency. Now considering the subject with reference to expediency only, let us examine whether it is safer to be a Christian or an infidel. Suppose that the two persons, one a Christian, and the other an infidel, to be closing their earthly existences. And suppose the infidel is right, and the Christian is wrong; they will then after death be upon an equality. But instead of the infidel being right, suppose him to be wrong, and the Christian right; then will the state of the latter after death be inestimably superior to that of the other.... And if you will examine the history of mankind, it will be plain that Christianity contributes much more to happiness in this life than that of infidelity. Now having briefly glanced at this subject, to what decision are we forced on the mere ground of expediency; certainly it is the adoption of Christianity. Having made our selection of Christianity, the next point is to consider whether we can believe the teachings of the sacred volume; if so, then, its adoption should of necessity follow, [sic] I have examined the subject maturely, and the evidence is very conclusive; and if we do not receive the Bible

as being authentic and credible, we must reject every other ancient work, as there is no other in favor of which so much evidence can be adduced.[140]

Interesting developments occurred. Not only was Jackson a Christian, but he was also making rational arguments for the existence of the faith. The mere presence of life and death mattered and, according to Jackson, might awaken a lost soul to Christ. He rightfully argued for the historical relevance and accuracy of the Scriptures. With the canon of Gospels and the entire canonization of the Bible being documented, supported by a reliable timeline in history, Stonewall argued that the Bible was to be as trusted as any other piece of historical evidence or writing. While perhaps surprising to the modern-day reader, the Bible's place in history and authenticity endured attacks similar to the ones of today. It would be a grave error to assume Christianity dominated the states in the 1800s. The atheist today was the "infidel" of the past, and there were many. Jackson argued for divine authority and inspiration from the Scriptures as the WCF similarly teaches in 1.4:

> The authority of the Holy Scripture, for which it ought to be believed, and obeyed, dependeth not upon the testimony of any man, or church; but wholly upon God (who is truth itself) the author thereof: and therefore it is to be received, because it is the Word of God.[141]

Jackson's affirmed belief in the Scriptures was necessary for any disciple of Christ. Additionally, being well read in history, he ascertained the importance and historical reliability of the canonization of the Bible.

Conclusively, the role of the professor provided benefits in Jackson's life. The position brought stability and an opportunity to grow in both wisdom and knowledge. The professor made intelligible Christian and philosophical arguments that hold true today. He also practiced his faith, tithing ten percent of his earned wages.[142] Many of his letters to his sister reference God and even seem to allude to the fact that Jackson was teaching or sharing the tenets of Christianity. From analyzing the previous correspondences, Laura appeared to be aware of Christianity, but lacked Christian influence and culture. In one note, Jackson wrote, "O Sister, if you would only pray! If you would only become religious! I derive much pleasure from morning walks, in which is to be enjoyed the pure sweetness of caroling birds."[143] Another similar letter stated: "Will you not have some faith in the prayers of a dying mother & brother? My dearest sister, do throw yourself into the hands of God. Throw yourself upon his mercy, repent of your sins and believe that the Father will accept your prayers, and forgive your transgressions, for the sake of his son's merits. Remember that he hath said that they who come unto him he will in nowise cast off."[144]

Jackson worried about Laura's spiritual atmosphere and continuously attempted to reassure her of Christianity and the importance of following the Lord. He underlined the importance of repentance, the necessary turning away from sin as described in the WCF 15.3:

> Although repentance be not to be rested in, as any satisfaction for sin, or any cause of the pardon thereof, which is the act of God's free grace in Christ; yet it is of such necessity to all sinners, that none may expect pardon without it.[145]

Was Laura a nominal (in name only) believer? Did she embrace universalism? Did she deny the faith? Or did she lack in her walk with God? The answer is unknown, though the fact that Jackson urged her to remember their mother and brother (Warren) supports the position that she remained absent of genuine faith in Christ. This also seems to have been the opinion of Anna, Jackson's second wife, who worried about Laura's extended family and the influences surrounding her. In an additional letter to his sister, Jackson repeatedly argued for Christianity:

VMI, Christian Growth, and Evangelism

> The passage of Scripture from which I derived such sufficient support, whenever applied is in the following words, "acknowledge God in all thy ways, and He shall direct thy paths." What a comfort is this! My dear sister, it is useless for men to tell me that there is no God, and that His benign influence is not to be experienced in prayer, when it is offered in conformity to the Bible. For some time past not a single day has passed by without my feeling His hallowing presence whilst at my morning prayers. I endeavor to live in accordance with the above passage which means as I understand it, in all thy ways acknowledge God and He shall take care of you in all respects. What better Protector can we desire than One who is Omnipotent, Omniscient and Omnipresent, and who hath promised that He will take care of us in all things, and in addition to all this, the pledge coming from One who cannot lie.[146]

There is no denying that Jackson's faith was strong. The man grew substantially in his beliefs, joyously affirming his Savior and sharing all he could about his Lord. Referring to the three "omni" theological terms asserts that Jackson knew that God was all-powerful, all-knowing, and all-present. Such thoughts and beliefs only profess the desire to submit to God's will and sovereignty on earth. Additionally, he knew God would never abandon him, constantly affirming His presence (Isa. 41:10).

In Jackson's ongoing correspondence with his sister, a genuine love for her continued, perhaps a bit of an older brother's concern for her spiritual life. She remained the only surviving member of the original family he once knew. Jackson loved Laura and rejoiced in his communication with her.

From his memories of his mother, grandmother, and aunts, to his continued relationship with his sister, he appreciated the women in his life. Always known as a respectful and honest man, his reputation with outsiders—more specifically with women—followed him. Anna wrote, "He was not naturally social, but he was a most genuine and ardent admirer of true womanhood; and no man was more respectful and chivalrous in his bearing towards the gentler sex."[147] She continued: "He never passed a woman either of high or low degree, whether he knew her or not, without lifting his cap, and he was never lacking in any attention or service that he could render. When a lady entered the room he always rose to his feet and remained standing until she was seated."[148]

It is in 1853 that the life of Jackson took a new turn; he found love. He married Elinor Junkin in August 1853. This brief marriage ended in tragedy with the death of his wife and newborn child. During his time at VMI, he married a second time—to Mary Anna, "Anna," from whom many quotes have been taken. The next chapter is dedicated to Stonewall's marriages and family life. As any believer knows, the unity of a man and woman in Christian marriage is of great importance in a disciple's life (Gen. 2:24). Accordingly, as this study focuses on the Christian testimony of Stonewall Jackson, it is only appropriate to dedicate an entire chapter to the union in marriage between Jackson and his soulmates. No greater love, other than that of the Lord Himself, exists for the believer than that of his spouse (Eph. 5:25).

1854–1861

While perhaps not his ideal appointment, Jackson's time in Lexington proved to provide stability and further growth in his faith and understanding of the Lord. He later recalled that Lexington felt like home and the place most dear to his heart. On his deathbed, he proclaimed, "Bury me in Lexington, in the Valley of Virginia."[149]

The decade he spent in Lexington was perhaps the most momentous of his entire life. Certainly, most people know Stonewall as a legendary military general serving the Confederacy in the Civil War, yet his time in Lexington tripled that of his service in the Civil War and established him as a respectable leader, family man, believer in Christ, and servant to his country and state. Jackson honorably served the United States of America during the Mexican-American War and at VMI for nearly fifteen years. Towards the end of Jackson's service at VMI, politics further separated the nation and even his state of Virginia. Such division started a clash that soon led to the Civil War.

Politics, however, played a role in a regional division and differing opinions among Americans. Politically, Stonewall was a Democrat. Dabney wrote, "This term in Virginia always had reference more to the principles of Federal polity, the assertion of the sovereignty and reserved right of the States, and the strict limitation of those of the Central Government."[150] Going back to the debate between Federalists and anti-Federalists, the nation slowly drifted apart on state vs. federal rights. Dabney continued, "The State Constitution of South Carolina, the most thoroughly democratic of all the States as to Federal politics, is the farthest removed from literal democracy."[151] On Jackson's political mindset, the following is presented:

> It is probable that Jackson would have accepted the name of a Democrat in more of its literality than the statesmen we have described. In Federal politics, he was certainly a strict constructionist of the straightest sect. He voted with his party uniformly. To political discussions, in conversation, he was not given; and while exceedingly exact in maintaining candor, he would usually content himself, when assailed by a political opponent, with a firm and polite declaration that he could not concur in his opinions, relapsing then into a silence from which no pertinacity could tempt him.... His political opinions were, therefore, very far from being the echo of other men's. He approached each subject from his own point of view, and this was usually found to be as conclusive as it was original.[152]

According to those who knew him best, Jackson was not highly political. He would read the Bible or other books rather than political journals or political readings. Biographer James Robertson Jr.

commented, "He was an avid reader who enjoyed military narratives, especially volumes on the wars of Napoleon Bonaparte."[153] Perhaps, like the reader today, he held some positions dear to his heart and had his own opinions on issues but did not consume his life around politics or political discourse. While he did love Virginia, it is abundantly clear that the Scriptures remained more important to him. The Great Commission, and ultimately reaching souls for Christ, lay deeply imbedded in his heart.

As the years progressed with his time at VMI, he continued to evangelize and encourage his sister in faith. In 1854 he penned, "I hope that by the time you receive this that your health will have much improved. But my sister, be that as it may, do turn to God, and obey the teachings of the Bible. If you do not believe its teachings at least obey its doctrines and I believe that God will give you faith. Make but the effort and resolve to do what it teaches to the close of life, and then you may expect death to be disrobed of its terrors."[154] As in the years before, Jackson remained concerned with his sister's spiritual life and salvation. Sharing such concern for his sister's faith, he wrote to his aunt, "I wish that Laura was here. I want you dear Aunt to make her one of the number for whom you regularly pray. What answer did she give you in regard to your very kind and Christian letter to her. Pray that the Glorious work of grace here may go on. Laura appears to be blest with unusual good health this summer."[155] It is comforting that he never gave up on his sister. He always encouraged her and sought others to pray for her. Stonewall lived by prayer. The WSC inevitably influenced Jackson on prayer:

> Q. What rule hath God given for our direction in prayer?
>
> A. The whole word of God is of use to direct us in prayer; but the special rule of direction is that form of prayer which Christ taught his disciples, commonly called the Lord's prayer.[156]

As the years progressed, Jackson's understanding of Scripture grew, as did his desire to obey his Lord and Savior. Anna recounted one further change, "After he became a Christian he set his face against all worldly conformity, giving up dancing, theater-going, and every amusement that had a tendency to lead his thoughts and heart away from holy things."[157] Clearly, Jackson took verses such as Romans 12:2 to heart: "And be not conformed to this world: but be ye transformed by the renewing of your mind, that ye may prove what is that good, and acceptable, and perfect, will of God." Anna further explained, "Stonewall abstained from the use of all intoxicating drinks from principle having a fondness for them, as he himself confessed, and for that reason never daring to indulge his taste."[158] Anna then later recalled, "During the war, when asked by a brother officer to join him in a social glass, he replied, 'No, I thank you, but I never use it; I am more afraid of it than of Federal bullets.'"[159] Similarly, he decried tobacco. Jackson took the Scriptures literally and sought to glorify the Lord in his body (1 Cor. 6:19–20, 10:31).

John Esten Cooke best described Jackson's years at VMI as a time of "religion and family." In fact, Cooke noted that Stonewall was a "fatalist," or in more simple terms, "one that believed strongly in God's providence and the will of God."[160] The reality is that nothing occurred in life without the will of God. This mindset was the foundation of Jackson's worldview. Cooke reported, "Religious duties soon became the controlling occupation of his life; the society of good men and women his chief relaxation and greatest source of pleasure,[161] again emphasizing Jackson's motto: "Do your duty and leave the rest to God."[162] Such effort to live for the will of God brought forth an unusual strength of course.

On one occasion, Jackson disciplined a cadet who faced expulsion and was later terminated from the academy. This student sought to take revenge and kill the major. A fellow cadet explained the details of the coming attack and urged Jackson not to walk on his normal path. Jackson responded, "Let the assassin murder me if he will!"[163] The event unfolded: "As he approached the spot indicated, he saw the young man standing and awaiting him. He turned and gazed fixedly at him with that look which had fronted, unmoved, the most terrible scenes of carnage upon many battlefields. The youth could not sustain it; he lowered his eyes, and turning away in silence, left the spot, while Jackson calmly pursued his way."[164]

Jackson's reputation as a stern, powerful figure endured. Jackson vehemently taught that when his days ceased on earth, it would be at the hands and timing of God, and nothing could stop that from occurring. Stonewall Jackson believed in divine providence. The WSC explains providence:

> Q. What are God's works of providence?
>
> A. God's works of providence are his most holy, wise, and powerful preserving and governing all his creatures, and all their actions.[165]

Theologian Charles Hodge further explained: "The providence of God is thus seen to be universal and to extend to all His creatures and all their actions."[166] Providing an example, he added, "Men in sickness, in danger, or in any distress pray to God for help. This is not irrational. It supposes God's relation to the world to be precisely what it is declared to be in the Bible."[167] He concluded, "The Scriptures, the history of the world, and almost every man's experience bear abundant evidence to such divine interpositions."[168]

Additionally, Jackson was never late to church. He attended two services each Sunday and taught two Sunday school classes, one for white children and the other for African Americans.[169] A Sabbath school for slaves and blacks, which was initially founded in 1845, preoccupied much of Jackson's free time. The original school suffered greatly in attendance, but Jackson took over leadership, and its growth excelled, becoming re-established around 1855. In one letter to his Aunt Neale, the passion for his faith and promotion of education is evident:

> The subject of becoming a herald of the cross has often seriously engaged my attention, and I regard it as the most noble of all professions. It was the profession of our divine Redeemer, and I should not be surprised

were I to die upon a foreign field, clad in ministerial armor fighting under the banner of Jesus. What could be more glorious? But my conviction is that I am doing good here, and that for the present I am where God would have me be. Within the last few days, I have felt an unusual religious joy. I do rejoice to walk in the love of God...My Heavenly Father has condescended to use me as an instrument in getting up a large Sabbath-school for the negroes here. He has greatly blessed it, and I trust, all who connected with it.[170]

Several elements of this letter require an explanation. First, Aunt Neale was a relative from his mother's side. If the reader will recall, Jackson's mother was a devout Christian, never ceasing in her faith. Her family had a reputation for walking with God and taking the Lord's ways seriously. We can only imagine the joy the Neale family experienced when reading that their nephew was in Christ, seeking to please Him in all he did. Second, Jackson continued to submit to God's will. His passion for the battlefield and field service continued to be showcased by his own pen. Nevertheless, he submitted to the Lord's authority and providence, which meant a classroom teaching position for which he inarguably lacked zeal. Lastly here, for the first time, the reader gains additional insight into Jackson in his adult years regarding slavery or the treatment of African Americans.

We can say that Stonewall genuinely felt led to educate slaves. Indeed, one might view this as demeaning in itself, as the need to educate enslaved people should not have been a debate or service in the first place. Nevertheless, in the 1850s, education was not a right for any Virginian slave or African American: Whites even lacked education, as known from the childhood of Jackson. Of interest is Jackson detailing precisely how his Sabbath school ran in the following correspondence to another church member:

> Dear Sir, In compliance with your request I proceed to give you a statement respecting the condition of the Lexington Colored Sabbath School. But in

doing so, I feel it unnecessary to say more than a few words, as you are already acquainted with its leading features. The school is usually opened by singing part of a hymn, which should be announced the previous Sabbath. This is followed by reading one or more verses from the Bible, with explanations & applications; this is succeeded by prayer. After this each class is instructed by its teacher from the Bible, Catechism and hymn book. At the close of the school, which is near forty-five minutes from the opening, there is a public examination on two verses of the child catechism, published by our Board. These verses should be announced the previous Sabbath. After the close of the examination, the school is dismissed, the remaining part of the opening hymn having been sung immediately after the examination.... The system of reward you are acquainted with, and the premiums so far have been near a dozen Testaments and one Bible. The day of their presentation is the first Sabbath of each month. Several scholars are studying the shorter Catechism at the present time. Each teacher keeps a class book in which is noted each scholar's deportment in school. The lesson should be taught one Sabbath, with a view to examination & mark on the next. Each teacher at the close of the month gives me a circular (blanks having been furnished) exhibiting for each scholar the manner in which the lesson has been prepared, the conduct in school, no. of lates, absences, &c. From these circulars, I make a monthly entry in the record book, which contains not only the no. of lates & absences, but also the names of the teachers, scholars, owners, persons with whom the scholars are living, the lates & absences of teachers, and a weekly record of the proceedings of the school. By reference to the record book, I find 91 to be the no. of scholars there reported. Praying that the S. school convention may be a great blessing to the cause & to yourself I remain your attached friend.[171]

Stonewall viewed slaves and African Americans as children of God. Jackson felt that all races made up the body of Christ. While he could not comprehend the institution of slavery, he accepted it and maintained that African Americans were children of God and needed to hear the gospel. Biographer John Richardson added that in the Sabbath School, Jackson "led in the prayers, the Bible teaching, and the Catechism. He served in this capacity from its organization in 1855 until he entered the Confederate Army in 1861."[172]

Biographer Farwell wrote, "With his usual energy he canvassed slaveowners in the area and prodded free blacks influential in the black community to attend themselves or to send the children."[173] He added, "Although attendance was not compulsory, Jackson kept careful records and regularly paid visits to the owners of backsliders."[174] To partake in or run such a school directly violated Virginia law. Anna remarked on this school, "His interest in that race was the instruction of the colored people of Lexington. His interest in that race was simply because they had souls to save, and he continued to instruct them with great faithfulness and success up to the breaking-out of the War."[175] The Great Commission undoubtedly remained the priority for Jackson: "And Jesus came and spake unto them, saying, All power is given unto me in heaven and in Earth. Go ye therefore, and teach all nations, baptizing them in the name of the Father, and of the Son, and of the Holy Ghost: Teaching them to observe all things whatsoever I have commanded you: and, lo, I am with you always, even unto the end of the world. Amen" (Matthew 28:18–20).

Whether reaching out to his sister or educating Sunday school classes, Jackson was passionate about the Scriptures. He eventually practiced, learned, and memorized the Westminster Shorter Catechism. Then in 1858, Stonewall received an encouraging letter from his sister, which brought excitement and great joy to him. He responded to her most joyfully:

Stonewall Jackson: Saved By Providence

My Dear Sister, Your very welcome letter of last week reached me this morning and I am rejoiced to learn that you are so much concerned about "the one thing needful." I have never believed that you would be lost. I have borne in mind that our sainted mother's prayers would not be forgotten by our Heavenly Father. Though dead, her prayers, I trusted would be precious in the sight of the Lord. You wish to know how to come to God; so as to have your sins forgiven, and to receive "the inheritance which is incorruptible and undefiled, and that fadeth not away." Now my dear sister the way is plain: the savior says in Mark XVI Chapter, 16th verse "He that believeth and is baptized shall be saved." But you may ask what is it to believe. To explain this I will quote from an able theologian, and devoted servant of God. To believe in the sense in which the word is used here, "is feeling and acting as if there were a God, a Heaven, a Hell; as if we were sinners and must die; as if we deserve eternal death and were in danger of it. And in view of all, casting our eternal interests on the mercy of God in Christ Jesus. To do this is to be a Christian." You speak of having done all that you know in order to be accepted: this is too apt to be our error. We must not depend on making ourselves holy: but just come to the Father and ask him to forgive our sins for the sake of Jesus and rely entirely on the merits of Christ for our prayer being answered. The Father loves the Son and for his sake pardons those who plead the Son's merits....We should never think of presenting any merits of our own for we are all sinners. Do not trouble yourself too much about not having repented enough for your sins, for your letter shows that you have much concern about the subject. But let me advise you simply to do as God enabled me to do, that is, resolve to spend the remaining part of life in His service, to obey the teachings of the Bible until death, and to rely entirely on the mercy of God for being saved, and though the future looked dark, yet it has become very bright. Never despair, even old Christians have dark moments. Never omit to pray at regular times. For years your salvation has been my daily prayer and shall continue so. Write to me often and tell me all your trials, that I may be able as an instrument in the hands of God of doing something for your eternal welfare.[176]

Analyzing such a response is astonishing. Jackson's prayers, evangelism, and perseverance in Christ had paid off. Laura, clearly convicted, sought the Lord's will. Jackson continued to encourage and instruct her. One can only imagine his genuine excitement when receiving such correspondence. It is widely known in this study that, on her deathbed, Jackson's mother prayed for the salvation of her living children. To have the ability to spend eternity with her children with their Father in Heaven was the greatest reward she could have ever imagined. Jackson indeed felt similar sentiments. At the end of the letter, he continued to guide Laura, explaining the basic tenets of faith and reassuring her that salvation is never earned; it is a free gift from God. Theologian Charles Hodge supported Jackson's position: "The imperative question remains, How shall a man be just with God? If our moral excellence be not the ground on which God pronounces us just, what is that ground? The Bible and the people of God with one voice answer, "The righteousness of Christ." Every believer relies for his acceptance with God, not on himself but on Christ, not on what he is or has done, but on what Christ is and has done for him."[177]

Salvation is by faith alone and received from the grace of God. This did not mean that Laura was permitted to sin openly, but her works held no merit in her salvation. A genuine conversion centered on faith and produced "good works," but only from the regeneration of the soul, or the process known as election, and then sanctification.

Regeneration of the soul, the mere ability of performing any "good work" is attributed only to the Holy Spirit in the regenerated believer:

> Their ability to do good works is not at all of themselves, but wholly from the Spirit of Christ. And that they may be enabled thereunto, beside the graces they have already received, there is required an actual influence of the same Holy Spirit, to work in them to will, and to do, of his good pleasure: yet are they not hereupon to grow negligent, as if they were not bound to perform any duty unless upon a special motion of the Spirit; but they ought to be diligent in stirring up the grace of God that is in them. (WCF 16.3)[178]

Obedience to the Word of God and the Lord Himself remains possible only with the indwelling of the Holy Spirit (John 14). The Christian never must boast in good works, as God awakens the soul and works in the sinner's life.

Towards the end of his employment at VMI, Jackson experienced an unfamiliar task. He was called to supervise cadets on a military mission. The known abolitionist John Brown and his followers murderously attacked and occupied an arsenal of weaponry before being overtaken by Colonel Robert E. Lee. Brown, a Calvinist like Jackson, fought vigorously to end slavery by use of force, including sneak and deadly attacks on slavery proponents. VMI superintendent, Francis Smith, quickly volunteered his students and staff to the Virginia governor to assist in this situation. Staff members and some eighty cadets presented themselves at Harpers Ferry, where Jackson oversaw the artillery regiment and witnessed the execution of Brown. Historian J. Steven Wilkins accounts from Dabney's records of Jackson's words: "I was much impressed with the thought that before me stood a man, in the full vigor of health, who must in a few minutes be in eternity. I sent up a petition that he might be saved. Awful was the thought that he might in a few moments receive the sentence 'Depart ye wicked into everlasting fire.' I hope that he was prepared to die, but I am very doubtful—he wouldn't have a minister with him."[179] Jackson had little else to say about Brown's situation other than that he appeared to be a fanatic with whom he disagreed.

It is clear from those who knew Jackson that he disagreed with slavery and had a special place in his heart for African Americans. Though his reasons were unknown, and of particular peculiarity to Jackson, God allowed slavery to exist for one reason or another. Perhaps again, best understood and explained from the worldview of Jackson, is that the Lord soon also endeavored to end slavery.

The execution of John Brown soon led to further debates, discourse, and a nation's separation. The latter part led Jackson to another vocation, one that he preferred: becoming a soldier of war. Robertson summarized Jackson's reputation and service at VMI best: "Jackson entered a new and alien world at VMI. The military was all he knew. The complexities of simple society were beyond his knowledge."[180] He added: "Second, the overwhelming majority of stories, allegations, and anecdotes relative to Jackson came from fourth- and third-classmen: youngsters prone to exaggerate. The tales were also first impressions that lingered until the rudiments of leadership Jackson sought to instill in them finally took root. As often as not, those young cadets who most ridiculed Jackson became officers who begged to serve under his command in War. They laughed at him in one decade; they died for him in the next."[181]

Jackson struggled as a professor at VMI. The students, frankly, disliked him. However, the reader must know that several young men respected him and cared for him, though they were certainly not the majority. Either way, his reputation and service at the institute played an interesting role in the future of the Civil War. Several of the young men he taught, including many who disliked him, soon followed the future general into battle and would proudly give up their life for him.

Conclusion

Appointment at the Virginia Military Institute provided Stonewall Jackson with stability, a family, and a more passionate relationship with Jesus Christ. The position which he perhaps frowned upon most in his life really solidified him as a person, husband, leader, and warrior of Christ. While he struggled immensely in gaining the respect of the cadets at the time of their studies, these same men later referred to him as the greatest general the South had ever known.

Perhaps Jackson's passion remained not in the classroom at VMI but in the Sabbath school classes he instructed and in his personal studies of Christ completed at home. His studies grew his faith and provided him with an impressive argument for the existence of Christ, the canonization of Scripture, and detailed theological accounts and understanding. While the previous chapters might have left the reader uncertain of Jackson's faith or growth in Christ, the ten years he lived in Lexington provided clarity regarding his relationship with Jesus Christ.

The late general was a saint who sinned, far from perfect. However, he sought God's will and direction. Most importantly, he took to heart the Great Commission. While being a professor and man of military might, he shared the gospel. He educated children, both white and black, in God's Word and the Westminster Catechisms. He encouraged those who needed it, constantly reminding them that Jesus is the only way to eternal life.

Chapter 4

❖

Marriage and Family Life

WITHIN TRADITIONAL ORTHODOX Christian teachings, the marriage between believers is a sacred unity. After devotion to the Lord Himself, the spouse of a Christian holds a special place in the disciple's heart. The Bible makes such a declaration clear in the book of Genesis: "Therefore shall a man leave his father and his mother, and shall cleave unto his wife: and they shall be one flesh" (2:24). Analyzing the home life, including the marriages, of Stonewall Jackson remains essential in understanding the man better and examining his walk with the Lord Jesus Christ.

Stonewall spent a decade of his life (1851-1861) teaching at the Virginia Military Institute in Lexington, Virginia. While professorship dictated his life and career, he also raised a family during this decade. Jackson married twice. He suffered the loss of his first wife, Ellie, and child in childbirth. He also endured the death of another child early in his second marriage.

Lexington proved to be home. Undeniably, Stonewall held a special place in his heart for Lexington as his family and faith grew in this Virginia town. It also further developed his connection to Virginia and the region surrounding VMI. His loyalty was to the Lord, his family, and Virginia. This chapter pays particular attention to the family of Stonewall Jackson, including his spouses and their connection to Christianity. However, most important is Stonewall's continued growth, or "sanctification," and his unbroken desire to walk with the Lord. Comparable to other times earlier in his life, Jackson endured much pain and suffering; however, because of his faith and reliance on Christ, he persevered, submitting to the will of God.

First Marriage 1853

Jackson married Ms. Elinor "Ellie" Junkin on August 4, 1853. Ellie, the daughter of Rev. Dr. George Junkin and Julia Miller Junkin became at that time the most important part of Stonewall's life, outside of his growing relationship with Jesus Christ. Joyously, Ellie loved the Lord too, and the young Jackson couple began a marriage and spiritual journey together that stayed with Jackson for the remainder of his life. Anna, Jackson's second wife, shared the following about Ellie: "Remembered by all who knew her as a person of singular loveliness of character; as possessed of a great natural intelligence, which was developed in a family of high cultivation; while her native modesty and conscientiousness ripened, under parental culture, into a beautiful type of Christian womanhood."[182]

Jackson and Ellie met through his and her father's (Rev. Dr. Junkin) relationship. The men maintained one essential common trait: both practiced Christianity. Likewise, both were members of the Presbyterian faith. Dr. Junkin came from a well-established line of Scottish Covenanters. There is no doubt that Dr. Junkin served as a spiritual mentor to Jackson. In addition to being a Presbyterian minister, he served as Washington College's president. The two men befriended one another, often discussing theology.[183] This continued growth in Jackson's Christian walk is not unusual for the believer. Such a keen interest in the faith rests upon the convert's soul, leading to the desire for more knowledge of the Scriptures and the Lord. Presbyterian William S. Plumer argued, "The longer men live, and the more they live to the honor of their Master, the brighter shall be their crown in heaven."[184]

Jackson and Ellie became better acquainted at church, where they both taught Sunday school lessons. Ellie was the second oldest of five children and knew her Scriptures well. Her parents clearly embraced rearing up a child in the Lord's ways (Prov. 22:6). On her faith, Stonewall's nephew, Thomas Jackson Arnold, noted, "Her religious faith, having the simplicity of a trustful child, made her one of the sunniest, happiest of beings. This brightness of temper, and a calm, clear judgment, Eleanor inherited from her lovely mother; and these gracious qualities made Margaret (her sister) the more dependent on her sister."[185] Margaret, or "Maggie," remained the most important character in Ellie's life outside of her parents. Maggie later had her own legacy, being known as the Poet of the Confederacy.

Over time, Stonewall realized with the help of friends (Mr. and Mrs. D. H. Hill) that he was falling in love with Ellie. Not all in her family entirely welcomed this news—most prominently Maggie who remained protective of her younger sister.[186] Stonewall courted Ellie, and both agreed to marriage plans, though Ellie likely temporarily called this off because of the tension and lack of support from Maggie, whom she considered her best friend. After some time, Ellie regretted her decision; she continued the courtship of marriage secretly and proceeded with marriage. Biographers note that the courtship initially surprised the Junkin parents, but they nevertheless approved of the arrangement.

The couple married, and like many newlyweds, conflict ensued. Though a seemingly minor incident, a disagreement between the young couple occurred during their honeymoon in Quebec. Jackson and Ellie disagreed passionately on the logistics of the Sabbath. On a Lord's Day (the Sabbath day, or Sunday) in which Jackson sought to attend an artillery show by the nearby forces, Ellie maintained this broke the Sabbath rule-keeping. The decision to attend such a show infuriated Ellie. Oddly, but not entirely surprisingly, Maggie had accompanied the young couple on their honeymoon and agreed with Ellie. This occurrence ultimately led to a search for an understanding on Sabbath principles for Jackson. This situation did not dissolve, as upon returning to Virginia, Jackson became educated on the importance of "keeping the Sabbath." One particular book made an impression—*The Principles of Courtesy* by George Winfred Hervey.[187] Biographer Byron Farwell commented:

The courteous virtues—gentleness, cheerfulness, humility, et.al.—were examined, and specific instructions were offered for the proper observance of the Sabbath, the correct posture at prayer, the seemly manner of singing hymns. Rules were set forth governing the proper development when attending weddings and funerals, when making visits to the poor, and when smoking: in the city only: in the company of chimney's, on a fire-proof roof; [sic] in the country only "far from all human haunts."[188]

The reader today may view such convictions as odd or not with the time. However, Jackson strongly embraced orthodox or original Presbyterian teachings. The very confessions he studied and revered taught one to honor the Sabbath and keep it holy:

Q. How is the Sabbath to be sanctified?

A. The Sabbath is to be sanctified by a holy resting all that day, even from such worldly employments and recreations as are lawful on other days; and spending the whole time in the public and private exercises of God's worship, except so much as is to be taken up in the works of necessity and mercy. (WSC)[189]

This Sabbath is then kept holy unto the Lord, when men, after a due preparing of their hearts, and ordering of their common affairs beforehand, do not only observe an holy rest, all the day, from their own works, words, and thoughts about their worldly employments and recreations, but also are taken up, the whole time, in the public and private exercises of his worship, and in the duties of necessity and mercy. (WCF 21.8)[190]

If Jackson claimed to be a confessional Presbyterian, such an issue was paramount. Interestingly, the debate on the guidelines, or use of the Westminster Standards separated theologians, even in the days of Jackson. Presbyterians in the United States were divided in what we now commonly refer to as the "Old School" versus "New School" debate. One of the primary disagreements centered on adherence to the Confessions. Not surprisingly, figures such as Dabney, White (Jackson's pastor), and Jackson himself fell into line with the "Old School" Presbyterians, who were considered the more conservative branch. Most adherents in this branch argued that the Confessions were essential to the faith and an asset for Christian living. While acknowledging that they were not God's inspired Word, they pointed people to the Bible and the expectations of the Lord found in the sacred Scriptures.

Honoring the Sabbath was not legalistic at all, as Reformed theology constantly emphasized the need to obey the Lord in the "moral law." While theologians commonly agree that Jesus satisfied Jewish laws with His death on the cross, disagreements remain on the practice of the Sabbath and what laws Jesus' death and resurrection abolished. Within Presbyterian thought (Reformed theology) remains the Old Covenant and New Covenant. The WCF 19.5 explains:

> The moral law doth forever bind all, as well justified persons as others, to the obedience thereof; and that, not only in regard of the matter contained in it, but also in respect of the authority of God the Creator, who gave it. Neither doth Christ, in the gospel, any way dissolve, but much strengthen this obligation.[191]

Presbyterians historically embraced the concept of the moral law and earnestly believed that such doctrines remain intact. A leading Presbyterian at the time, William S. Plumer wrote, "If God makes laws for his rational creatures, they are bound to study them, and learn what they mean. This is implied in nearly every verse of the one hundred and nineteenth Psalm."[192] The following questions and answers in the WSC provide an understanding on the moral law:

> Q. What is the duty which God requireth of man?
>
> A. The duty which God requireth of man is obedience to his revealed will.
>
> Q. What did God at first reveal to man for the rule of his obedience?
>
> A. The rule which God at first revealed to man for his obedience was the moral law.[193]

Certainly, Presbyterians believe the death of Jesus provides the forgiveness of sins for all believers. However, analyzing such verses as John 14:15 and Matthew 22:36–40, Presbyterians teach that those who are in Christ seek to worship and follow Him in their heart, soul, and mind.

They are not working for salvation, they are walking with their Lord in this fallen world (Luke 9:23–24). WCF 19.6 further states the following:

> Although true believers be not under the law, as a covenant of works, to be thereby justified, or condemned; yet is it of great use to them, as well as to others; in that, as a rule of life informing them of the will of God, and their duty, it directs and binds them to walk accordingly; discovering also the sinful pollutions of their nature, hearts, and lives; so as, examining themselves thereby, they may come to further conviction of, humiliation for, and hatred against sin, together with a clearer sight of the need they have of Christ, and the perfection of his obedience. It is likewise of use to the regenerate, to restrain their corruptions, in that it forbids sin: and the threatenings of it serve to show what even their sins deserve; and

Marriage and Family Life

what afflictions, in this life, they may expect for them, although freed from the curse thereof threatened in the law. The promises of it, in like manner, show them God's approbation of obedience, and what blessings they may expect upon the performance thereof: although not as due to them by the law as a covenant of works. So as, a man's doing good, and refraining from evil, because the law encourageth to the one, and deterreth from the other, is no evidence of his being under the law; and, not under grace.[194]

Jackson, a fairly new Presbyterian, strengthened his position on the idea of Sabbath-keeping. For him, he recognized the errors in his previous thinking and later declared, "Were this day intended to be observed as a season of bodily renovation and repose, then whatever could contribute to this object would be allowed. But it is especially for the weary enslaved soul that this day is ordained to be hallowed. If we examine Isaiah's exposition of this command, we will find it requires us to abstain from every thought, word and action which affords gratification to a worldly mind."[195]

Such a growth in faith is impressive. His desire to glorify his Lord and Savior remained clear. Ellie clearly assisted in some type of spiritual maturity and understanding within Jackson's life. His marriage to Ellie and place in the Junkin family provided his first experience of becoming part of a firm Christian Bible-believing extended family.

Surprisingly, not everyone apparently knew of their marriage. Most shockingly, Jackson's sister, Laura, remained out of the loop. His nephew, Thomas Jackson Arnold, remembered a visit from the newlywed couple:

> I distinctly remember the visit of the uncle and his wife the following summer of 1854, to the home of my parents (Laura and husband), and how all the family were delighted and charmed with the uncle's bride. It

would seem that Miss Junkin had exacted a promise from Major Jackson to disclose to no one the fact of the contemplated marriage, which she intended should be a surprise to all except her immediate family; in his strict conception of the sanctity of his word he extended the obligation to include his sister, and the failure to inform her of the expected event proved a sore wound to her feelings, and one that was slow in the healing.[196]

As his nephew mentioned, Laura remained hurt that Stonewall had kept the courtship a secret. However, in analyzing the letters from Jackson to his sister, modern-day biographers note she should have noticed from "hints" and insinuations that marriage was inevitable. While biographers say the incident strained their relationship, the siblings' relationship endured. In one letter correspondence to Laura, Jackson wrote of Ellie (now his wife):

I send you a lock of Ellie's hair; this she reluctantly parts with because of its color, which she hopes proves more acceptable to your taste than it has ever been to hers. My message to you is that you must prize it very highly as being the token of a sister's love and from a brother's wife. Send us a lock of your hair, and also one from Grace [niece]. Tell her to give me the prettiest she has, so that I may look at it when I am so far off that I cannot see her pretty face. Tell her furthermore that I have told her aunt that Grace is very pretty, and her conduct must be as good as her face. Ellie joins me in love to you and the family. Your Brother, Thomas.[197]

In another letter exemplifying his Christian worldview, Jackson shared of the death of his mother-in-law.

> We have recently been called to mourn the death of my mother-in-law. She, without any apparent uneasy concern, passed into that unseen world, where the weary are at rest. Her life was such as to attract around her many warm friends, and if she had any enemy in this world, it was and continues to be a secret to me. Hers was a Christian life, and hers was a Christian death. She had been afflicted with rheumatism for several months previous to the close of her life, and on Saturday preceding her death she had the return of a malady which had formerly afflicted her.... She said that she was not afraid to die, and that she found Jesus precious in her soul. When asked by one of her daughters what they should do without her, she replied that the Lord would provide. She was strongly attached to her family and they to her; yet she appeared to have no concern about what would become of herself or family, such was her complete confidence in the promises of the Bible. She felt assured that God would provide for her family, and she felt that she was going to her Saviour, with whom she expected to enjoy unending happiness. She asked us to kiss her and told her children to live near Jesus and to be kind to one another. Her death was no leaping into the dark. She died in the bright hope of an unending immortality of happiness.[198]

Jackson had a similar deathbed experience with his own mother—focused on the peace of being with the Lord and the will of God emerged. Both mothers surrendered their worldly lives to embrace the passing as God's will and enthusiastically looked forward to being in their Lord's presence. While no longer a boy, Stonewall clearly remained affected by such testaments. Plumer wrote on the ultimate peace in death of a Christian: "God has promised eternal life—a conscious, happy existence—to all who love his Son and keep his commandments."[199] He later warned that "no one can be fit to die who does not hate every false way, who does not turn from all sin, and lay fast hold on the merits of the Redeemer."[200]

While not nearly the number of records or writings exist in his first marriage to Ellie compared to his wedlock with Anna, there are enough testimonies to ascertain that Ellie's Christian influence on Jackson was strong, never-ending and, at times, challenging. His walk with the Lord deepened. On a stronger devotion to prayer life, he later penned:

> I have so fixed the habit in my own mind that I never raise a glass of water to my lips without lifting my heart to God in thanks and prayer for the water of life. Then, when we take our meals there is grace. Whenever I drop a letter in the post office, I send a petition along with it for God's blessing upon its mission and the person to whom it is sent. When I break the seal of a letter I have just received, I stop to ask God to prepare me for its contents and make it a messenger of good. When I go to my classroom and await the arrangement of the cadets in their places that is my time to intercede with God for them. And so in every act of the day I have made the practice habitual.[201]

Jackson welcomed the concept of an active, personal Savior in Jesus Christ. He spoke directly to his Lord through prayer. As the years continued, everyone knew Jackson as a man of prayer. The habit increased throughout his life, being one of his most deciding and fundamental practices. On describing prayer, Charles Hodge taught, "As prayer, in the Scriptural sense of terms, includes all converse with God whether in the form of praise, thanksgiving, confession, or petition, all the ascriptions of glory to Christ, as well as all direct supplications addressed to Him, come under his head."[202]

Similarly, from those who knew Jackson best, his opinion radically changed on the act of war. He decided that he personally would never enter another conflict unless it were a "defensive war." He also remained clear that he would not seek commission into the US Army because of the same sentiments. Original biographers often called Jackson a "professor of religion." Such a transformation is unsurprising. The morality of war shook his being, enabling him to contemplate the seriousness of such destruction. Without question, Jackson increasingly embraced the Christian worldview in all aspects of life. The late military historian G. F. R. Henderson wrote, "He took the Bible as his guide, and it is possible that his literal interpretation of its precepts caused many to regard him as a fanatic."[203] While some may have described Jackson as a fanatic, the truth is, he merely believed the Bible. His position was supported by the WCF 1.10:

> The supreme judge by which all controversies of religion are to be determined, and all decrees of councils, opinions of ancient writers, doctrines of men, and private spirits, are to be examined, and in whose sentence we are to rest, can be no other but the Holy Spirit speaking in the Scripture.[204]

Perhaps surprising again to the reader is the false idea that the people of the 19th century practiced Christianity with stronger conviction than today's generation. Nominal believers dictated much of the nation, as did the concept of cultural Christianity. Several decades later, the infamous Scopes Trial shocked the country, ultimately solidifying the fact that not all "Christian" Americans embraced the teachings of Christ nor the literal interpretation of the Scripture. Rest assured, however, there remains a powerful body of Christ, both in Jackson's time and even today, that would not cease in their admiration and belief in the historical doctrines of Christianity. Further supporting the notion of Jackson's newly embraced Sabbath tradition, Henderson added: "His observance of the Sabbath was hardly in accordance with ordinary usage. He never read a letter on that day, nor posted one; he believed that the

Government in carrying the mails were violating a divine law, and he considered the suppression of such traffic one of the most important duties of legislature."[205]

Jackson sought to obey and respect Jesus. The man, a sinner like all humanity, remained far from perfect. However, his reliance on the Scriptures and the Lord's direction underlined his faith. While described as a fanatic by some, his preferred label was *a follower of Jesus Christ*. "My sheep hear my voice, and I know them, and they follow me" (John 10:27). On following Christ, Presbyterian minister Benjamin Morgan Palmer taught, "Submission is the personal homage which, in the full consciousness of our own individuality, we render to the will of a supreme loving Father. And until it is reached as the final and habitual posture of our hearts, there remains the necessity for continued discipline until every thought is brought into captivity to the obedience of Christ. Happiest they who can earliest say: Thy will, my God, Thy will be done, And let that will be mine."[206]

Sadly, Jackson's first marriage ended abruptly after only fourteen months. Ellie went to be with the Lord while delivering a stillborn daughter.[207] Clearly, such an event challenged the faith of Jackson. R. L. Dabney wrote, "The memorials of his short connection with this accomplished lady are scanty; but enough is known to show that he was a tender husband."[208] He continued, "It is related that his grief was so pungent, as not only to distress, but seriously to alarm his friends. Yet even then he was most anxious not to sin by questioning in his heart the wisdom and rectitude of God's dealing with him."[209]

Certainly, Jackson regularly experienced losing loved ones so dear to him. Undoubtedly, his soul hurt, and depression followed. Jackson was a quiet man, often reserved in his thoughts, yet his relationship with Christ clearly assisted him in such heartache. Anna wrote, "For a long time he visited her grave daily, always stood over it with uncovered head, absorbed in tender and loving memories."[210] His Christian worldview faced a new obstacle, one which Dabney remarked made him initially more prone to worldly practices. Nevertheless, this was only temporary, as he held firm to his faith as accounted in a letter written to his aunt, Mrs. Neale:

Your kind letter, so full of sympathy and love, made a deep impression on my stricken heart. I can hardly realize yet that my dear Ellie is no more that she will never again welcome my return no more soothe my troubled spirit by her ever kind, sympathizing heart, words and love.... She has left me such monuments of her love to God, and deep dependence upon her Saviour's merits, that were I not to believe her happiness, neither would I believe though one were to rise from the dead and declare it. God's promises change not. She was a child of God, and as such, she is enjoying Him forever. I have suffered so much with my eyes lately that I have had great fears that I might lose them entirely, but all things are in the hands of a merciful Father, and to His will I hope ever cheerfully to submit.[211]

Reassuring is the fact that Jackson remained with his Lord and Savior. Evidently, he submitted to the will of God. Without question, this must have been an awful experience he could not fathom or understand. Left widowed and experiencing death from personal relatives again, a common occurrence in his young life continued. However, Ellie, a strong Christian, made her mark on Jackson's life. She alone influenced his position on the Sabbath and surrendered her life to the Lord and His ways. Ellie played a role in the growth of Jackson, one that continued with him until his death. The reader must acknowledge the positive influence of Christian women in his life.

His health issues intensified, causing much pain and worry to those who loved him most. One cadet, Thomas M. Boyd, journaled the burial of his wife: "With cap in his hand, he stood beside the open grave. He was extremely pale but calm and resigned. He did not shed a tear, yet everyone who saw him was impressed with the intense agony he was enduring. In a day or two he was back at his post, pursued his even, quiet, regular life. He had grown paler, but beyond this, and the bit of crepe on his cap and the handle of his sword, no one would have known the severe ordeal through which he had passed, nor the bitterness of that intensely passionate soul."[212]

After several conversations with dear friends, Jackson agreed to take a leave from Lexington and embark on a European tour. Dabney wrote: "During this season of discipline, his health suffered seriously, and his friends induced him, in the summer of 1856, to make a European tour, in the hope that the spell might be broken which bound him in sadness. He visited England, Belgium, France and Switzerland, spending about four months among the venerable architectural remains, and before mountain scenery of those countries."[213]

In a letter to his sister, Laura, Jackson wrote of the time abroad as necessary: "You are a very kind and affectionate sister, yet even with you I would be reminded of the loss of happiness which I once enjoyed with dear Ellie. So I have to some extent torn myself away from that state of mind which I feared, should my summer have been passed at home or in the United States."[214]

During his time in France, he picked up the language and often read the Scriptures in French upon his return home. Anna concluded regarding his visit abroad, "The great object of his journey attained. Aside from the pleasure of seeing foreign countries, his health was perfectly restored, and he was ready to resume his work."[215] Dabney wrote, "He returned from this holiday with animal spirits and health completely renovated. Although he resorted no more to society, he resumed scientific occupations with zest, and his religious life again became as sunny and cheerful as was his wont."[216] The trip undeniably benefitted his physical ailment, but, most impressively, his spiritual well-being was restored.

Second Marriage 1857

On July 16, 1857, Stonewall married a second time. This marriage was to Mary Anna "Anna" Morrison. As a young lady from North Carolina, she knew Jackson even while he was married to Ellie. She and her sister lived in Lexington, where they were acquainted with the Jackson family through common friends. Anna joyfully recalled how Jackson often escorted her sister and her to church.[217] The military leader had an interest in her, ultimately leading to a marriage proposal. In sharing the news of his engagement and invitation to the wedding, Jackson wrote to sister Laura: "I will tell you that Miss Mary Anna Morrison, a friend of mine, in the western part of North Carolina, and in the Southern part of the state, is engaged to be married to an acquaintance of yours living in this village, and she has requested me to urge you to attend her wedding in July next. To use her own words, she says, 'I hope your sister will come. You must come.'"[218]

Anna came from an established family and was the daughter of a pastor, like Ellie had been. Anna described her father: "My father, the Rev. Dr. H. H. Morrison, a Presbyterian minister, had in his earlier life been a pastor in towns, and was the first president of Davidson College, in North Carolina; but his health having failed, he sought a country home for rest and restoration, and reared his large family of ten children principally in this secluded spot, where he was able to preach to a group of country churches."[219] Her mother was Mrs. Mary Morrison (Graham), the daughter of General Joseph Graham and sister of William A. Graham, governor of North Carolina, US Senator, and Secretary of the Navy.[220] Anna and her family were Christians and of the same denomination as Jackson.

For the second time, Jackson married in the faith, uniting in bond to a fellow believer, which is a direct command found in the Bible. "Be ye not unequally yoked together with unbelievers: for what fellowship hath righteousness with unrighteousness? and what communion hath light with darkness?" (2 Cor. 6:14). The WCF 24.3 also plainly teaches the following:

> It is lawful for all sorts of people to marry, who are able with judgment to give their consent. Yet it is the duty of Christians to marry only in the Lord. And therefore such as profess the true reformed religion should not marry with infidels, papists, or other idolaters:

neither should such as are godly be unequally yoked, by marrying with such as are notoriously wicked in their life, or maintain damnable heresies.[221]

Although Jackson wrote letters often to Laura, his sister, Jackson's writings to his wife, Anna, provide a unique insight into his character. Known as a famous, strong-willed, daring military figure, yet, when examining his written correspondence, Jackson is recognized as a family man with strong faith. Sharing some of their letters, Anna thought of Jackson as the most tenderhearted gentleman:

> April 25, 1857. It is a great comfort to me to know that although I am not with you, yet you are in the hands of One who will not permit any evil to come nigh you. What a consoling thought it is to know that we may, with perfect confidence, commit all our friends to Jesus to the care of our Heavenly Father, with an assurance that all will be well with them!

> May 7, 1857. I wish I could be with you tomorrow at your communion. Though absent in body, yet in spirit I shall be present, and my prayer will be for growth in every Christian grace. I take pleasure in the part of my prayers in which I beg that every temporal and spiritual blessing may be yours, and that the glory of God may be the controlling and absorbing thought of our lives in our new relation.

> May 16, 1857. There is something very pleasant in the thought of your mailing me a letter every Monday; such manifestation of regard for the Sabbath must be well-pleasing in the sight of God. Oh that all our people would manifest such a regard for his holy day! If we would all strictly observe his holy laws, what would not our country be?[222]

The writer produces only a select portion of the letters here to focus on the Christian exchanges and declaration of faith. Impressively, Jackson consistently concentrates on Christ, even referring to the Sabbath conviction thoroughly discussed in the study. Remarkably, Stonewall continued to grow in his knowledge and understanding of Christianity. From expressing interest in Christ to a devout Presbyterian, Jackson persevered as a follower of the Lord.

Clearly, the duo maintained a firm foundation built on a joint declaration to live and serve Christ. The couple honeymooned in Niagara Falls, New York. Biographer Byron Farwell wrote that upon their return, "in January 1858 the Jacksons moved into a comfortable two-story house of stone and brick with an English half basement on Washington Street in downtown Lexington. It was the only house Jackson ever owned, and he was destined to enjoy it for less than three years."[223] In this home, it remained abundantly clear, the family sought to serve the Lord (Josh. 24:15). Anna recalled:

> A few months after our marriage he proposed that we should study together the Shorter Catechism as a Sabbath-afternoon exercise, and it was not long until we committed it to memory—he reciting it to me with perfect accuracy from beginning to end. This he had not been taught in his youth, although he had read it carefully before committing himself to Presbyterianism. He considered it a model of sound doctrine, as he did also the Confession of Faith; but his chief study was the Bible itself, which was truly a lamp unto his feet, and a light unto his path.[224]

Presbyterians, like other Protestant Christians, openly refer to themselves as Bible-believing Christians. However, orthodox Presbyterians refer to themselves also as confessional. This entails an agreement with the Westminster Standards—Confession of Faith, Larger Catechism, and Shorter Catechism. In such documents exist a declaration of beliefs on Scripture, reaffirming their position on controversies and establishing their distinct beliefs in teachings separate from the Roman Catholic Church. Most church historians acknowledge that three of the oldest Protestant denominations are Lutherans, Reformed adherents, and Presbyterians. Jackson proudly embraced *sola Scriptura*, or Scripture alone, yet also viewed the Westminster Confession and Catechisms as tools to further strengthen his position and knowledge of the Bible. WSC Q&As 2 and 3 teach the following:

> Q. What rule hath God given to direct us how we may glorify and enjoy him?
>
> A. The Word of God, which is contained in the Scriptures of the Old and New Testaments, is the only rule to direct us how we may glorify and enjoy him.
>
> Q. What do the Scriptures principally teach?
>
> A. The Scriptures principally teach what man is to believe concerning God, and what duty God requires of man.[225]

The Jackson home undisputedly remained structured to glorify the Lord. Dabney commented on such practices found in the house: "His family prayers were held at seven o'clock, summer and winter, and all his domestics were rigidly required to be present."[226] Anna acknowledged the custom: "He required all servants to attend promptly and regularly. He never waited for anyone, not even his wife."[227]

Prayer and family worship were integral parts of family life. Family worship, embraced more openly in past generations, is a simple yet foundational aspect of Christian living. The concept is essential: the man of the house reads the Scriptures, and the family studies and discusses the presented passages. Further, most families sing hymns and psalms and pray.

Here again, the writer addressed the servants, or the slaves, who lived with the Jackson family. Anna explained: "The first slave he ever owned was a man named Albert, who came to him and begged that he would buy him on the condition that he might be permitted to emancipate himself by a return of the purchase-money, as he would be able to pay it in annual installments. Major Jackson granted his request, although he had to wait several years before the debt could be paid, and my impression is that it was not fully paid when the war broke out."[228] She recalled another: "The next servant that came into his possession was an old woman, Amy, who was about to be sold for debt, and who sought from him a deliverance from her troubles. This was some time before our marriage, when he had no use for her services, but his kind heart was moved by her situation and he yielded to her entreaties and gave her a home in a good, Christian family, until he had one of his own."[229]

Anna herself owned four slaves, including "Miss Hetty and her two boys."[230] Anna's parents transferred the first three to the Jackson family upon her marriage to Stonewall. The two boys, named Cyrus and George, were eventually educated by Anna. "I taught them to read, and he required them to attend regular family worship, Sunday-school, and church. He was a very strict but kind master, giving to his servants that which is just and equal, but exacting of them prompt obedience."[231] Another young girl, Emma, became the servant of Anna.[232]

Biographer Richard G. Williams Jr. commented: "As one who took the Scriptures literally, Jackson was mindful that God was concerned about how he treated his servants and fellow man. Since Jackson knew that he would one day have to answer to his Master, he desired to be treated mercifully, and he knew he could expect no better treatment than he exhibited: 'Masters, give unto your servants that which is just and equal; knowing that ye also have a Master in heaven' (Colossians 4:1)."[233]

As Jackson's marriage continued, so did his letters to Laura. On one occasion, he referenced the fact that Laura seemingly grew in Christian faith and understanding. He remarked, "For years your salvation has been my daily prayer and shall continue so."[234] In another letter, he wrote:

> I thank our heavenly Father for having given you that peace which passeth all understanding, and which the

world can neither give nor take away. The world may wrong us and deceive us, but it never can take from us that joy resulting from an assurance of God's love. You may expect dark hours, but never for one moment permit yourself to despond. The followers of Christ are expressly told in the Bible that in this life they shall have tribulation; but our Saviour has also told us to be of good cheer, for He has overcome the world; which teaches us that if we but persevere in the ways of welldoing that we also shall overcome the world.[235]

Jackson's reassurance of salvation and direction from the Lord only encouraged Laura further. Here, he served not only as an older brother, but also as a spiritual mentor on her Christian journey.

As in his first marriage, pregnancy came fast. Anna gave birth to a daughter, Mary Graham, on April 30, 1858. Devastatingly, the young infant suffered from jaundice and died on May 25, not living for even one month. Expecting her death, Jackson penned to Laura, "Our little daughter is very ill of jaundice, and she may at any hour take her place among the redeemed in Paradise."[236] Responding to a condolence letter from his young niece, Jackson confirmed the death of Mary Graham:

My Dear Little Niece: Your very interesting letter reached me a short time before your sweet little cousin and my little daughter was called from this world of sin to enjoy the heavenly happiness of Paradise. She died of jaundice on May 25. Whilst your Aunt Anna and myself [sic] feel our loss, yet we know that God has taken her away in love. Jesus says, "Suffer little children to come unto me, and forbid them not, for of such is the kingdom of heaven." Did you ever think, my dear Grace, that the most persons who have died and gone to heaven are little children? Your aunt is doing very well; she is out visiting. We hope to go and see you all this summer, but my health is so delicate that I am disposed to go North first.[237]

In experiencing the death of his infant child, Jackson's response resembles King David's in the Scriptures, relying on the fact that his child is in heaven (2 Sam. 12:23). The WCF 10.3 teaches the following:

> Elect infants, dying in infancy, are regenerated, and saved by Christ, through the Spirit, who worketh when, and where, and how he pleaseth: so also are all other elect persons who are incapable of being outwardly called by the ministry of the Word.[238]

Believing these Standards, Jackson understood that the infant or young child of a believer upon death is in heaven. The familiar verse that is used and supported by Jackson teaches, "But when Jesus saw it, he was much displeased, and said unto them, Suffer the little children to come unto me, and forbid them not: for of such is the kingdom of God" (Mark 10:14). In this verse, the Lord clearly shows that children are unique in the sight of God and separated from adults. Jackson's knowledge of Scripture was impressive and theologically sound. Of note is that the couple had another daughter, Julia Laura Jackson, born in 1862 when the nation was at war.

In 1859, the Jacksons headed to New York for Anna to receive treatment for her medical issues. Jackson always sought the most well-known and established doctors to care for his wife. In a letter to Laura referencing Anna's health worries, he wrote, "I am very thankful to see you bear up under your trials with such Christian fortitude, and as long as we lean on His Almighty arm, all shall be well. I reached home on last Friday night about three o'clock in the morning. Anna is an invalid still, but I trust that better health is in store for her."[239] Repeatedly, Jackson showed submission to God's providence. Undeniably, he prayed for his ill wife but held assurance that she was a believer and remained destined to be with the Lord in this life or the next.

Eventually, Jackson needed to return to Virginia while Anna stayed in New York for a short time. She shared some letters he composed during this time of separation:

> May 7, 1859: You must not be discouraged at the slowness of recovery. Look up to Him who giveth liberally for faith to be resigned to His divine will and trust Him for that measure of health which will most glorify Him and advance to the greatest extent your own real happiness. We are sometimes suffered to be in a state of perplexity, that our faith may be tried and grow stronger. All things work together for good to God's children. See if you cannot spend a short time after dark in looking out of your window into space, and meditating upon heaven, with all its joys, unspeakable and full of glory; and think of what the Saviour relinquished in glory when he came to earth, and of his sufferings for us; and seek to realize, with the apostle, that the afflictions of the present life are not worthy to be compared with the glory which shall be revealed in us.[240]

> August 15, 1859: Last night I enjoyed what I have long desired listening to a sermon from Rev. Dr. Thornwell, of South Carolina. He opened with introduction, setting forth the encouragements and discouragements under which he spoke. Among the encouragements, he stated that the good effected here would be widely disseminated, as there were visitors from every Southern State. Following the example of the apostle Paul, he observed that whilst he felt an interest in all, yet he felt a special interest in those from his own State. He spoke of the educated and accomplished audience it was his privilege to address. After concluding his introductory remarks, he took

his text from Genesis, seventeenth Chapter, seventh verse, which he presented in a bold, profound, and to me original manner. I felt what a privilege it was to listen to such an exposition of God's truth. He showed that in Adam's fall we have raised from the position of servants to that of children of God. He gave a brief account of his own difficulties when a college student, in comprehending his relation to God. He represented man as a redeemed being at the day of judgment, standing nearest to the throne, the angels being farther removed. And why? Because his Brother is sitting upon the throne he is a nearer relation to Christ than the angels. And his being the righteousness of God himself. I don't recollect having ever before felt such love to God. I was rather surprised at seeing so much grace and gesture in Dr. Thornwell. I hope and pray much good will result from this great exposition of Bible truth.[241]

Both letters are evidence of tremendous spiritual growth and maturity. Such rhetoric and references to God were not the standard in his day. Examining his walk with and dependence on the Lord in every aspect of his life, he persevered in his faith. The WCF 13.1 states the following on the concept of sanctification:

> They, who are once effectually called, and regenerated, having a new heart, and a new spirit created in them, are further sanctified, really and personally, through the virtue of Christ's death and resurrection, by his Word and Spirit dwelling in them: the dominion of the whole body of sin is destroyed, and the several lusts thereof are more and more weakened and mortified; and they more and more quickened and strengthened in all saving graces, to the practice of true holiness, without which no man shall see the Lord.[242]

The execution of John Brown in 1859 shook the nation and further divided the abolitionists and promoters of the Confederacy. It is telling that Jackson needed to decide the future of his allegiance. Would this famed war veteran defend the nation from separation from the only country he had ever served, or would he remain loyal to the state he called home? Jackson chose the latter option, disappointing his extended and close family, including his sister, Laura. The following chapter analyzes his decision.

Conclusion

All humanity suffers from trials and tribulations. The death of immediate loved ones remained a regular occurrence in Jackson's life. The man, once an orphan, experienced more suffering than those around him. His home life had never been stable until he met Anna. His first wife, Ellie, died prematurely in childbirth delivering their first child. This produced great hurt and devastated his soul.

Thankfully, Jackson found love again in marriage with Anna, yet they too lost their first child. Jackson's faith and reliance on the Lord persevered and grew through all the hardships. From his letters, actions, and accounts by those who knew him, he served the Lord foremost in his life.

Unfortunately, slavery cannot be erased from his legacy. Though by all accounts, he was kind to his servants. He cared for their souls and salvation. This is clear by his promotion of education and shared prayers with them. He took the Scriptures to heart, noting the command to treat slaves fairly and kindly.

He was a man of his time, living in a unique part of history, one in which the context must be understood. Jackson was far from perfect; Jackson himself would acknowledge that. Sin remained present, producing a constant battle between the spirit and flesh. Jackson rejoiced that the Lord Jesus saves souls of those who fall to their knees before Him, seeing their sin and clinging to their Savior, and then seek to walk with Him in this fallen world.

Chapter 5

❖

SECESSION AND THE BEGINNING OF THE CIVIL WAR

THE NATION REMAINED divided in the 1860s, like many other times in United States history. While it is true that the concept of abolitionism grew in the North, the role and size of the government continued to be questioned within a large part of the nation, in particular, the South. Many Southerners became increasingly alarmed when President Abraham Lincoln took office.

Known from his debates with Senator Stephen Douglas, Lincoln disliked slavery. But, he repeatedly said he would not interfere with States where slavery already exisisted and he had no right to do so. For most Southerners, however, slavery was not the only factor in secession from the Union. Others viewed the growing federal government as a direct threat to individual statehood. We can argue that Virginia, Jackson's home state, took this position.

The following questions remain when studying the causes of the Civil War: Was the secession of the South correlated to slavery, and slavery only? Or did the southern states, led by South Carolina, leave the Union because of exploitation and potential interference by the Republican Party? Such questions and answers continue to divide Northerners, Southerners, and historians still today. One side viewed a united Union as a constitutional requirement while the other viewed separation as a constitutional right. Whether one took a position of separation, the brewing conflict could no longer be ignored. The United States of America remained divided, both politically and characteristically.

It would be an error and highly irresponsible to declare that every Southerner fought for the institution of slavery. The South comprised a variety of opinions on slavery; many viewed the institution as a state-versus-federal issue. Some had no firm opinion on slavery yet fought for their home state. It is fair to classify Stonewall Jackson in this last category. While Jackson did own slaves and was historically connected to the institution by extended family, his loyalty remained to the state of Virginia. Many merely fought for the side where they geographically lived. From those who knew Jackson best, he did not agree with the institution of slavery, yet felt his providential God allowed the practice. This chapter addresses secession and the early combat experiences of Jackson while mainly focusing on his Christian worldview, even in times of turmoil, including battle.

Secession 1860

The raid of John Brown in the fall of 1859 led the way for one of the last conflicts between abolitionists and pro-slavery proponents. Around a year later, in December 1860, South Carolina formally left the Union, breaking up the once stable United States of America. The election of Abraham Lincoln angered many Southerners, leading to further separation in political beliefs. The State of Virginia, well aware of a potential crisis, enabled legislation that placed the cadets and staff at VMI under the state's military order. Biographer Byron Farwell wrote, "When the Virginia General Assembly met after the John Brown's raid, it passed a new militia act which, among other items, formally recognized the VMI officers as a part of the state's military establishment and placed the cadets in the service of the state, under the military command of those appointed to govern. Jackson and the other senior professors were appointed majors in the Corps of Engineers."[243]

Virginia remained separated, with many in the northern part of the state siding with the Union in maintaining a united nation.

Secession and the Beginning of the Civil War

Moreover, the state realized it needed its own militia to protect its territory from any upcoming engagement, anticipating an uneasy relationship with the federal government.

South Carolina started the secession movement in 1860; several states followed. Virginia, a divided state, was one of the last to secede. Not surprisingly, the geographical location played a factor here. The eventual creation of the state of West Virginia signifies the division in Virginia regarding Union loyalty. Jackson's hometown and his sister Laura's home were, in fact, in West Virginia, although the military leader had spent the last ten years of his life in Lexington, a place he considered home and a location that inarguably affected his views on secession and state rights. Perhaps expecting Virginian secession, Jackson penned the following to sister Laura on December 29, 1860: "I am looking forward with great interest to January 4 when the Christian people of this land will lift their united prayer incense to the Throne of God in supplication for our unhappy country. What is the feeling about Beverly respecting secession? I am anxious to hear from the native part of my state. I am strong for the Union at present, and if things become no worse, I hope to continue so. I think that the majority in this country are for the Union, but in counties bordering on us there is a strong secession feeling."[244]

It may surprise some that Jackson wanted to preserve the Union, prompting the question: What possibly led Jackson to eventually change his mind? First, he noted, "at present." While politically aware of his nation's government, Jackson did not dedicate his leisure to political discourse. However, he did firmly believe that states should maintain individual rights, a principle that had long been established in Virginia by the original Founding Fathers. Virginians were unique, and most followed in the individual footsteps of liberty from George Washington, Thomas Jefferson, and James Madison. Lastly, Jackson briefly mentioned the counties bordering him that favored secession. Jackson's home was in Lexington, a place in the middle of Virginia before West Virginia ever existed. Employment at VMI, often described as West Point in the South, played a role in Jackson's beliefs and thoughts on Virginian loyalty. Appointed as an officer of the state in 1860,

Jackson's allegiance decision was perhaps made for him. Of course, he could have resigned from VMI and left for the north, but this decision would have altered his life and placed him in an almost foreign land as his home was in the South and also most of his family and friends. Understandably, home for Stonewall Jackson meant Virginia.

The State of Virginia observed all events unfolding before deciding on secession. Stonewall biographer Roy Bird Cook commented on Virginia's final decision, "On April 17, Governor John Letcher refused to obey Lincoln's call for troops, and on the same day the Virginia Convention repealed the ordinance by which it had adopted the Constitution of the United States and seceded from the Union."[245] In a similar way to Jackson's letter to Laura, Anna Jackson explained that he initially strongly supported a unified Union: "At this time Major Jackson was strong for the Union, but at the same time he was a firm States-rights man. In politics he had always been a Democrat, but he was never a very strong partisan, and took no part in the political contest of 1860, except to cast his vote for John C. Breckenridge, believing that his election would do more to save the Union than that of any other candidate. He never was a secessionist and maintained that it was better for the South to fight for her rights in the Union than out of it."[246]

A question fair to propose is: Why then did Jackson side with the Confederacy if he felt secession was not in the country's best interest? While South Carolina was the first to leave the Union, several other states followed. This domino effect did not sit well with those in power in Washington DC. In the view of President Lincoln, a rebellion ensued. He ordered the unseceded States to provide 75,000 troops to suppress "illegal combinations" in the South.[247] Such a declaration angered those in Virginia. Jackson was one of these figures who felt Lincoln's actions were unjustified. In the eyes of Virginians, Abraham Lincoln had just declared war on his own people—brothers, if you will—sharing ancestral heritage. Lincoln's opponents felt strongly that they maintained a constitutional right to secede if their federal government grew too strong or strayed in a direction they disliked.

Anna Jackson disclosed Stonewall's remarks to his pastor: "If the general government should persist in the measures now threatened, there must be a war. It is painful to discover with what unconcern they speak of war and threaten to it. They do not know its horrors. I have seen enough of it to make me look upon it as the sum of all evils."[248] He added, "Should the step be taken which is now threatened, we shall have no other alternative; we must fight. But do you not think that all the Christian people of the land could be induced to unite in a concert of prayer to avert so great an evil? It seems to me that if they would thus unite in prayer, war might be prevented and peace preserved."[249] Jackson's loyalty to Virginia is clear. His remarks distinctly underline the view that suggests, according to him, the federal government was unreasonable and would ultimately cause a deadly confrontation with any potential invasion of southern states, including his own Virginia. More telling, however, is that he exercised caution when speaking of war. Further, he sought peace through dedication to prayer.

While his reputation never kept him from excelling in combat situations, Stonewall Jackson had become a devoted man of God and had declared that he would never engage in another conflict unless it was in defense of his nation. Invading and occupying his home state of Virginia fell strictly within these boundaries, as he often alluded to the fact that the federal troops were "invaders." Fellow Presbyterian R.L. Dabney shared such a sentiment: "It is perfectly clear that sacred Scripture legalizes such defensive war. Abram, Moses, Joshua, Samuel, David, Josiah, the Maccabees, were such warriors; and they were God's chosen saints."[250] He added, "Our homes and the shelter of our families, the rights and all our fellow citizens, everything which is included as valuable in the words, my country, is committed to his protection."[251]

Consistent with his view of God's providence, Jackson considered secession as the will of God, emphasizing that it only came to fruition through divine providence.[252] Historian George C. Rable remarks, "Jackson naturally viewed the Civil War as a providential judgment against a sinful people."[253] WCF 5.2 addresses the providence of God:

> Although, in relation to the foreknowledge and decree of God, the First Cause, all things come to pass immutably, and infallibly; yet, by the same providence, he ordereth them to fall out, according to the nature of second causes, either necessarily, freely, or contingently.[254]

On providence connected to the government, Presbyterian Charles Hodge asserted:

> The idea that God would create this vast universe teeming with life in all its forms and exercise no control over it, to secure it from destruction or from working out nothing but evil, is utterly inconsistent with the nature of God. And to suppose that anything so minute as to escape His notice, or that the infinitude of particulars can distract His attentions, is to forget that God is infinite. It cannot require any effort in Him, the omnipresent and infinite intelligence, to comprehend and to direct all things however complicated, numerous, or minute.... God is as much present everywhere and with everything, as though He were only in one place and had but one object of attention.[255]

Jackson did, in fact, fight for Virginia and upheld his beliefs in state rights. History today teaches that the primary reason for the Civil War, or War between the States, was the abolition of slavery. However, convincing arguments exist that it was state rights that played the most significant factor in secession. Opinions differed on the issue of slavery being the fundamental conflict; even today, historians remain divided on the root causes of the struggle. Views on slavery separated the nation. Nonetheless, it is reasonable to recognize that most Southerners sided with Jackson in their battle against a growing powerful federal government. Further, the same people defended their states, homes and often the only land they ever knew. Anna addressed the topic in her own writing:

> It has been said that General Jackson fought for the slavery and the Southern Confederacy with the unshaken conviction that both were to endure. This statement is true with regard to the latter, but I am very confident that he would never have fought for the sole object of perpetuating slavery. It was for her constitutional rights that that South resisted the North, and slavery was only comprehended among those rights. He found the institution a responsible and troublesome one, and I have heard him say that he would prefer to see the negroes free, but he believed the Bible taught that slavery was sanctioned by the Creator himself, who maketh men to differ, and instituted laws for the bond and the free.

She added:

> He, therefore, accepted slavery, as it existed in the Southern States, not as a thing desirable itself, but as allowed by the Providence for ends which it was not his business to determine. At the same time, the negroes had no truer friend, no greater benefactor. Those who were servants in his own house he treated with the greatest kindness, and never was more happy or more devoted to any work than that of teaching the colored children in Sunday-school.[256]

As previously recorded, Jackson felt firmly that slavery remained at the will of his Lord and Savior. From Anna's remarks, some may argue that Jackson fought to maintain slavery; however, more than likely, the major disagreement he held was based on state versus federal rights, an original division of the Founding Fathers. In a letter to his nephew, Thomas Arnold, Stonewall wrote:

> I desire to see the state [Virginia] use every influence she possesses in order to procure an honorable

adjustment of our troubles, but if after having done so the free states, instead of permitting us to enjoy the rights guaranteed to us by the Constitution of our country, should endeavor to subjugate us, and thus excite our slaves to servile insurrection in which our families will be murdered without quarter or mercy, it becomes us to wage such a war as will bring hostilities to a speedy close. People who are anxious to bring on war don't know what they are bargaining for; they don't see all the horrors that must accompany such an event.... For myself, I have never as yet been induced to believe that Virginia will even have to leave the Union. I feel pretty well satisfied that the Northern people love the Union more than they do their peculiar notions of slavery and that they will prove it to us when satisfied that we are in earnest about leaving the Confederacy unless they do us justice.[257]

This discourse mentioned slavery and state rights. Opponents and promoters of slavery would use Jackson's words to defend their position, although most evidence suggests that Jackson firmly fought for his state of Virginia and their right to "independence." He emphasized state rights and alluded to the notion that Virginia would protect itself from a potential invasion.

Critical to evaluate are Lincoln's original thoughts on slavery. First, he said repeatedly that he would leave slavery alone where it existed and did not know what to do about it even if he had the power, which he did not have. Further, unknown to most people, is the fact that Lincoln even pondered relocating slaves to island territories or Africa. Southerners will acknowledge abolishment of slavery did not occur, until the war actually begun and lasted for several years.

It is fair to conclude, state rights laid at the core of a future clash. Regardless, Jackson prepared for war. The Governor promoted Jackson to colonel with the VMI cadets and staff under Virginia military control. People in Virginia knew the call for federal forces was not a threat but the beginning of a conflict. Jackson biographer John Esten Cooke wrote, "The passage of the ordinance of secession became known on the 18th, and on April 19, Lieutenant Jones, of the United States Army, evacuated Harper's Ferry, having first attempted to blow up the public buildings there."[258] By April 1861, Jackson knew his loyalty was with Virginia. Around two weeks before his departure to Harper's Ferry, he wrote to his sister:

> I am well satisfied that you are a child of God, and that you will be saved in Heaven, there forever to dwell with the ransomed of the Lord. So you must not doubt. The natural sun may never return to the view of the child of God, but the Son of Righteousness will. But there is one very essential thing to the child of God who would enjoy the comfort of religion, and that is he or she must live in accordance with the law of God, must have no will but His; knowing the path of duty must not hesitate for a moment, but at once walk in it. Jesus says, "My yoke is easy and My burden is light," and this is true, if we but follow Him in the prompt discharge of every duty; but we mustn't hesitate a moment about doing our duty, under all circumstances, as it is made known to us; and we should always seek by prayer to be taught our duty.... If temptations are presented, you must not think that you are committing sin in consequence of having a sinful thought. Even the Saviour was presented with the thought of worshipping Satan. What could be more abhorrent to a Christian's feelings than such a thought? But such thoughts become sinful if we desire pleasure from them. The devil injects sinful ideas into our minds to disturb our peace, and to make us sin; and it is our duty to see by prayer and watchfulness that we are not defiled by them.[259]

This is the last correspondence between Laura and Stonewall. The Civil War divided families, and here is proof of such assertions. Laura remained a staunch supporter of the Union and felt extremely disappointed in her brother's allegiance to the Confederacy. Often referred to as the conflict of brothers killing brothers, this scenario provides new insight into such claims. The only two remaining Jacksons from their parents' marriage separated. Sadly, this war divided families across the nation. Jackson always loved Laura, eventually naming his daughter after his younger sister.

In response to an order from operational headquarters, Jackson left Lexington, Virginia, for Harper's Ferry on April 27, 1861. Upon his arrival, Jackson caught the attention of onlookers, mostly because of his rugged appearance and lack of military insignia compared to other officers.[260] John Esten Cooke wrote, "The new colonel was a strong contrast to all this. He rode an old horse who seemed to have little of the romance of war about him, and nothing at all fine in his equipment."[261] Jackson knew the state of Virginia remained a dangerous stronghold and wrote to his wife that she should head to North Carolina to take residence with her father.[262] On the importance of Harper's Ferry, Anna wrote, "Harper's Ferry now became the rendezvous of all the troops in the Valley of Virginia, and it was the command of these and others sent to reinforce them that was given to Colonel Jackson when he received his commission in the service of Virginia."[263] Here at Harper's Ferry is where Jackson's infamous brigade formed. Cooke described, "The First Brigade as it was now called consisting of the 2nd Virginia, Colonel Allen; the 4th Virginia, Colonel Preston; the 5th Virginia, Colonel Harper, and the 27th [Lt-Colonel Echols commands], to which was soon afterward added the 33rd Virginia, Colonel Cumming."[264]

Writing in May 1861, Jackson wrote to Anna, "I am very thankful to an ever-kind Providence for enabling you so satisfactorily to arrange our home matters. I just love my business little woman [sic]. Let Mr. Tebbs have the horse and rockaway at his own price; and if he is not able to pay for them, you may give them to him, as he is a minister of the Gospel..... My habitual prayer is that our kind Heavenly Father will give unto my darling every needful blessing, and she may have that peace which passeth all understanding."[265] By June 14, 1861, Jackson noted he would leave the area soon as evacuations were underway.[266] In a June 18 letter, he penned to Anna, "I trust that through the blessing of God, we shall soon be given an opportunity of driving the invaders from this region."[267]

Viewing his service as a defender rather than the aggressor, Jackson's men in late June found themselves in a skirmish that resulted in the death of several men. He noted his "men were anxious for battle" and eagerly waiting to chase off the invading federal troops.[268] In early July, General Robert E. Lee wrote to Jackson, promoting him to brigadier general.[269] Understandably, Jackson did not know what the future held. One part of him thought the Confederates had the opportunity to chase the federal troops out of Virginia and end the conflict. However, he also knew his Providential God would ultimately decide all events about to occur, which ultimately was the beginning of the deadliest conflict in United States history.

BATTLE OF FIRST MANASSAS

The Battle of Manassas became the first significant victory for Confederate forces. Inarguably, it shocked the Union strategists and became the occurrence where Jackson earned his title "Stonewall," brilliantly showing his ability to hold firm under pressure, much like his time during the Mexican-American War. The nickname, said to have been given by General B. E. Bee, came as a result of Jackson "rallying his men in which the General declared, 'See, there stands Jackson like a stone wall!'"[270] The Battle of First Manassas is where Jackson's legend and reputation as a strong military leader resurfaced and continued until his death.

The battle was fierce, deadly, and devastating. To the onlooker, Jackson resembled a man unfazed by, or perhaps uncaring of, the immediate fire and deadly conflict developing around him. Those who knew the general were aware that this was not a heartless leader, yet one who remained calm in conflict and acted in cautioning emotion versus fear. Cooke shared the story: "General Bee remarked, 'General, they are beating us back!' The fact is Jackson betrayed no corresponding emotion. He had his war look on, but that was never a look of excitement. His eye glittered, and, in the curt tone habitual with him, he said coolly, 'Sir, we will give them the bayonet.'"[271] Bee died in the battle. Jackson resembled the dedicated warrior of a decade before during the Mexican-American War. Any war veteran would acknowledge that some fold under the pressure, and others excel; Jackson excelled in the high-stress situation of active combat, almost resembling the bravery and intelligence of King David found in the Bible (1 Samuel 17). Jackson single-handedly made a difference in a battle that seemed almost impossible to win.

Despite the two forces being virtually equally built, the Confederates won their first major battle, shocking Washington DC. Jackson's brilliant tactics and unwavering confidence assisted in that victory. When troops retreated, Stonewall reinforced the line, held a powerful position, and reengaged the enemy. The legend was born: a man never again to be underestimated on the battlefield. Cooke supported such accounts: "In the midst of this hot struggle Jackson's equanimity remained unshaken. He does not seem, during any portion of the battle, to have contemplated disaster or defeat, and opposed to the agitation and furry [sic] of many around him a demeanor entirely unmoved."[272] Cooke described Jackson's resiliency in this way:

> Jackson had held his position for about an hour, and this had enabled General Beauregard to hurry forward troops from the lines along Bull Run. These were at last in position, and taking command of them in person, General Beauregard, about three o' clock, ordered the whole line to advance and make a decisive assault. Jackson still held the centre, and, although wounded in the hand by a fragment of shell, paid no attention to the accident. At the word, his brigade rushed forward, broke through the Federal line in

front of them, and supported by reserves, drove the enemy from the plateau.[273]

From his years as an orphan to the engagements in Mexico, Jackson maintained bravery and discipline. As Jackson came to understand the providence of God, he was enabled to exercise courage that came from his Lord and Savior. Theologian Charles Hodge explained, "The Providence of God extends not only over nations, but also over individuals. The circumstances of every man's birth, life, and death are ordered by God."[274] Hodge expounded further:

> Whether we are born in a heathen or in a Christian land, in the Church or out of it; whether we are weak or strong, with many or few talents, prosperous or afflicted; whether we live a longer or shorter time, are not matters determined by chance, or by the unintelligent sequence of events, but by the will of God. "The Lord killeth, and maketh alive: he bringeth down to the grave, and bringeth up. The Lord maketh poor and maketh rich: he bringeth low and lifteth up." (1 Samuel 2:6–7) "My times are in thy hands." (Psalm 31:15)[275]

Jackson held such a position. This faithful peace relied on the will of God versus an unknown fate or destiny. If Jackson lived accordingly with the Lord, he felt comforted in whatever outcome Providence decided, whether it be death or life. Indeed, a stronger sense of bravery and fearlessness grew more potent with a deeper and more personal relationship with his Lord. WCF 5.5 attests to such an idea (emphasis added):

> The most wise, righteous, and gracious God doth oftentimes leave, for a season, his own children to manifold temptations, and the corruption of their own hearts, to

chastise them for their former sins, or to discover unto them the hidden strength of corruption and deceitfulness of their hearts, that they may be humbled; and, to raise them to a more close and constant dependence for their support upon himself, and to make them more watchful against all future occasions of sin, and for sundry other just and holy ends.[276]

Jackson's philosophical thought was simple. The strength he maintained was not his, yet the Spirit inside of him. He also knew well that if he died, his soul would enter heaven.

In sharing the news of his victory, Stonewall penned to Anna: "My Precious Pet, Yesterday we fought a great battle and gained a great victory, for which all glory is due to God alone.... The battle was the hardest that I have ever been in, but not near so hot in its fire. I commanded in the centre more particularly, though one of my regiments extended to the right for some distance. There were other commanders on my right and left. Whilst great credit is due to other parts of our gallant army, God made my brigade more instrumental than any other in repulsing the main attack."[277] Jackson rightfully acknowledged that the battle was the most difficult in his life. It was a battle that continues to be studied today by historians all over the world. Not surprisingly, from the beliefs of Jackson, all glory needed to be given to God for His deliverance in victory.

Seemingly answering Anna about her disgust of the papers not mentioning his role in the success, he replied: "As you think the papers do not notice me enough, I send a specimen, which you will see from the upper part of the paper is a leader. My darling, never distrust our God, who doeth all things well. In due time He will make manifest all His pleasure, which is all His people should desire. You must not be concerned at seeing other parts of the army lauded, and my brigade not mentioned. Truth is mighty and will prevail."[278] Jackson portrayed humility and humbleness (Prov. 11:2). Assuredly, he knew his victory was monumental and historically significant;

though consistent with his Christian character, he explained to Anna that the Lord was in charge of all affairs.

In a letter composed to Colonel J. M. Bennett, Jackson gave credit for the victory to his Lord and Savior: "Through the blessing of Providence, my brigade passed our retreating forces, met the thus far victorious enemy, held him in check until reinforcements arrived and finally pierced his centre, and thus gave a fatal blow."[279] Quoting a man that served with Jackson, Rev. John Richardson noted his reference to Jackson's view of providence:

> No man ever lived who seemed to have a more practical and living sense of his truth of Christianity. His belief in the control of the divine Providence was rational as well as Scriptural. He believed with all his heart that God exercised a special Providence over His children for their good and controlled all events for their welfare. He believed that no creature was mighty enough to resist God's power and none so feeble as to be neglected by His care. This conviction produced in him a courageous serenity. It made him both industrious and trustful. He never doubted for a moment the superintendence of God in the affairs of life.[280]

While the phrase "all glory to God" may be easy to declare, Stonewall lived it by continually acknowledging and praising his Savior. Faith in Christ clearly regenerated his heart and the indwelling of the Holy Spirit, produced such confidence. William S. Plumer wrote, "In the great change issuing in salvation, God thoroughly changes both man's state and man's heart, and brings him into the kingdom and under the government of the Son of his love. There is no change greater than this."[281] Jackson lived for his Lord's will, and the fruit of thankfulness and assurance grew. Jackson understood his life was not his own, yet he existed only to glorify his Savior. The WCF 16.2 explains this further:

These good works, done in obedience to God's commandments, are the fruits and evidences of a true and lively faith: and by them believers manifest their thankfulness, strengthen their assurance, edify their brethren, adorn the profession of the gospel, stop the mouths of the adversaries, and glorify God, whose workmanship they are, created in Christ Jesus thereunto, that, having their fruit unto holiness, they may have the end, eternal life.[282]

Late Summer to Winter 1861

While Jackson's remaining summer and fall months were relatively quiet, his fame and reputation grew, even reaching foreign lands. The war continued as far out as Missouri, and the conflict that was once expected to be brief proved it could be a long war with no clear victor in sight. In an August 1861 letter, Jackson penned to Anna, "Don't put any faith in the assertion that there will be no more fighting till October. It may not be till then; and God grant that, if consistent with His will, it may never be."[283] On September 26, Jackson summarized for his wife a sermon from R. L. Dabney:

His text was from Acts, seventh Chapter and fifth verse, he stated that the word of God being in italics indicated that it was not in the original, and he thought it would have been better not have been in the translation. It would have then read: Calling upon and saying, Lord Jesus, receive my spirit. He spoke of Stephen, the first martyr under the new dispensation, like Abel, the first under the old, dying by the hand of violence, then drew a graphic picture of his probably broken limbs, mangled flesh and features, conspiring to heighten his agonizing sufferings.... But in the midst of this intense pain, God, in His infinite wisdom and mercy, permitted him to see the heavens opened, so that he might behold the glory of God, and Jesus, of whom he was speaking, standing on the right hand of God. Was not such a heavenly vision enough to make him forgetful of his sufferings? He beautifully and forcibly described the death of the righteous, and as forcibly that of the wicked.[284]

R. L. Dabney, a well-respected Presbyterian pastor, camped with the Virginia soldiers before Manassas, saw the engagement himself during the battle, and took residence with Stonewall's brigade following the victory. He later became the Chief of Staff for Stonewall, yet during 1861, he served as a chaplain preaching to Confederate troops. Such sermons provided hope and an understanding of the realities of life and war.

For the rest of 1861, Jackson maintained a camp near Centreville, just outside the Manassas battle site. Here, his brigade endured the infamous discipline of Jackson, where no soldier was untested. They "marched, counter-marched and practiced military formation."[285] The soldiers constantly worked and engaged in drills. Jackson's reputation as a military perfectionist remained.

On Sundays, the brigade held two Sabbath services, practicing the observance of Jackson's tradition in Lexington.[286] One historian James Robertson Jr. noted, "As became his custom when unable to observe the Sabbath, he decreed the weekday [Monday] as the Lord's Day."[287] Anna wrote of the loyalty and respect the soldiers serving under Jackson had for Stonewall as a military commander and a Christian in sharing what one soldier declared, "Wherever the voice of our brave and beloved general is heard, we are ready to follow.… We do not look upon him merely as our commander, we do not regard him as a severe disciplinarian, as a politician, as a man seeking popularity but as a Christian; a brave man who appreciates the condition of a common soldier, as a fatherly protector; as one who endures all hardships in common with his followers; who never commands others to face danger without putting himself in the van."[288]

Stonewall demanded and expected the best from his men, but he loved them dearly. Those who knew him best described his love for the soldiers as that of a father-type bond. Civil War historian James I. Robertson Jr. similarly wrote, "Most of them [soldiers under Jackson] had never seen a man so dedicated to his God, and the spectacle of prayers and silent meditation by this warrior at all hours of the day and night had its humorous side. Yet just as Jackson's spirit of battle rubbed off on them, so too did his faith. Soon the brigade was as noted for its worship as its fighting. Wherever it camped, chapel tents were among the first to be pitched, and at frequent church services, Jackson himself acted as usher for his men."[289]

Undoubtedly, Jackson argued that a brigade dedicated to the Lord maintained an advantage. The Scriptures supported such logic with comparisons to ancient Israel, walking with or without the Lord. Each generation made its own decision, and Jackson resembled the person of Joshua, the elite warrior who sought his family and people to serve the Lord (Joshua 24). Jackson understood the impact his Christian faith could have on the outcome of battles. John Richardson expanded on Jackson's beliefs:

> Stonewall Jackson believed that the best soldier is the one who has made his peace with God and strives to do his duty day by day. The Christian soldier keeps morally clean. He is not found in the hospital with a venereal disease or in the stockade because of drunkenness. Instead of being a liability to his nation, he is an asset. Instead of weakening his outfit he strengthens it. Men need a strong Christian faith to properly motivate their conduct, and they find such motivation in Christianity. Jackson said he would like to command an army composed only of converted men. He felt this way because he had experienced the power of Christ in his own life. Let Stonewall Jackson ever be to us an example of the power of pure Christianity to make real men![290]

With new orders, Stonewall said his goodbyes to his brigade, one that fought earnestly with him and provided the Confederates with their first significant victory in the war. Jackson encouraged his brigade with the following words: "You have already gained a brilliant and deservedly high reputation throughout the army of the whole Confederacy, and I trust in the future, by your deeds on the field, and by the assistance of the same kind of Providence who has heretofore favored our cause, you will gain more victories, and add additional luster to the reputation you now enjoy."[291] Jackson's emotional farewell tugged at the hearts of the soldiers who had just shed blood with him.

For some, Jackson instilled a sense of hope and faith as he resembled the earnest reputation of a great Christian man, which challenged each individual to prioritize following the Lord in their own lives. Jackson's Christian testimony laid upon the hearts of many soldiers—believers and unbelievers—who served with him. Jackson gave all glory to God and trusted fully in God's sovereign grace. Plumer explained this action further, "Cast yourself and your endeavors wholly on God's great mercy in Christ Jesus. Seek to have yourself and your labors washed in atoning blood. Freely admit that you are nothing, that you deserve nothing, and that all you dare to hope to be and to obtain, is wholly through God's sovereign grace. Be humble."[292] Assuredly, Jackson's actions gave evidence of this. WCF refers to this as sanctification:

> They, who are once effectually called, and regenerated, having a new heart, and a new spirit created in them, are further sanctified, really and personally, through the virtue of Christ's death and resurrection, by his Word and Spirit dwelling in them: the dominion of the whole body of sin is destroyed, and the several lusts thereof are more and more weakened and mortified; and they more and more quickened and strengthened in all saving graces, to the practice of true holiness, without which no man shall see the Lord. (13.1)

> This sanctification is throughout, in the whole man; yet imperfect in this life, there abiding still some remnants of corruption in every part; whence ariseth a continual and irreconcilable war, the flesh lusting against the Spirit, and the Spirit against the flesh. (13.2)[293]

Chaplain W. W. Bennett also reflected on the impact of Jackson: "General Jackson gave every encouragement to religion among his soldiers; he was the model Christian officer in our armies, active, humble, consistent—restraining profanity and Sabbath breaking—welcoming colporteurs, distributing tracts, and anxious to have every regiment in his army supplied with a chaplain."[294]

Near the end of 1861, Jackson asked for prayers in a letter to Anna: "Continue to pray for me, that I may live to glorify God more and more, by serving Him and our country."[295] Jackson rightfully asked for spiritual guidance through prayers. Furthermore, he desired to glorify his Lord in all aspects of life. Lastly, his words acknowledged that the Confederacy was no longer just an idea, but a distinct land that he sought to defend; labeling the Confederacy as their country.

In another letter he also mentioned the servants living with Anna in Lexington: "I desire, if practicable, that my boys shall have the opportunity of attending the colored Sabbath-school in Lexington if it is still in operation."[296] He finally concluded: "Should you not need George, please hire him to some suitable-person, with the condition that, if in or near town, he be required to attend Sabbath-school; and wherever he may be, let him be required to attend church at suitable times, as I am very desirous that spiritual interests of my servants shall be attended to."[297]

Jackson loved these individuals. Jackson felt that every race made up the Kingdom of God. While such accounts are used to attack his nature and positions on slavery, they also prove that in a time of war and division, he cared deeply for the spiritual well-being of others. At the beginning of the war, Jackson's Christian worldview endured. From his correspondence with his wife, soldiers, and extended family, he always sought God's direction.

CONCLUSION

Accounts differ about why Jackson fought for Virginia. Some assert that it was to protect the institution of slavery. While some of his writings are controversial and perhaps supporting a slavery justification, from his own pen and from the mouth of others who knew him, Jackson did not openly support the practice of slavery. He did, however, firmly believe in state rights. Further, he held great appreciation and love for Virginia, the only home he truly ever knew.

Jackson seceded from the Union because his state did. He had faithfully served the United States of America and the Virginia Military Institute. He served the latter for ten years, holding Lexington as the dearest place to his heart. He sided with Virginia and his home. Once the Union troops engaged in invasion, Stonewall hesitated no longer and viewed the engagement as the defense of his nation (Confederate States of America) and homeland.

In battle, his reputation grew, only adding to his impressive legacy from Mexico. Jackson resembled the great warriors of King David and Joshua. His leadership and discipline unquestionably won the Confederates their first major battle, though from those who fought under him, his Christian character best described him. Jackson served the Lord first and surrendered to His will. Jackson believed that no battle or event in life existed without the providential guidance from his Lord and Savior.

Today, scholars often refer to the men of the famed Stonewall Brigade as a mighty Christian unit. Jackson's leadership and the Lord's providence uniquely formed such an organization, and carried over into the division and corps that he commanded. While all his men may not have been Christian, his impact on his men was everlasting, providing examples to countless souls for the years to come. The very life of Jackson served as a great Christian testimony to those men who served alongside him.

Chapter 6

❖

STONEWALL'S LAST YEARS 1862–1863

BY THE END OF 1861, the Confederate States of America became quite familiar with the person, fame, and reputation of General Stonewall Jackson. The general's fame reached other parts of the globe, most notably Great Britain. The Union, who once felt confident that the war would be over quickly and labeled it as an untimely rebellion, slowly learned that they had underestimated the Southern Army from the beginning of the conflict, suffering numerous casualties and defeats in many battles. The Confederates had reputable leaders serving as generals and other commanding officers, many educated at West Point just like their Union counterparts.

The Southerners, labeled as rebels, felt that action was justified, viewing the conflict as an invasion by the North. Stonewall fell into this category; he remained a proud Virginian and maintained that he was defending his homeland from federal invasion. From 1862 to 1863, the common theme is warfare. Jackson's military success and fame continued. He also endured several defeats. However, since the primary objective of this study is to analyze his Christian worldview, there is perhaps no better period during which to delve into such research. Questions remain: Did Stonewall Jackson maintain his Christian worldview in the most pivotal moments of the war? What impact did he have on others?

Sadly, Jackson died in 1863, wounded and eventually succumbing to death because of his injuries. Like his mother, he surrendered his will to the Lord and died peacefully. While the chapter will briefly address battle specifics, we emphasize Jackson's Christian faith, including his ultimate passing into Glory. A common idea appears and ends with Jackson grasping the Providential view of God. For Jackson, he was a mere tool in the ultimate plan of Jesus Christ. As is clear with his continued fame today, the general made an everlasting impact on the lives of others, one he would be most proud of with its connection to Christianity and providing all glory to that of his Lord and Savior, Jesus Christ.

1862

Jackson's long-lasting fame was secured during his Valley Campaign of March-June 1862. Now a Major General, his 15,000 men defeated three larger federal armies and frightened Washington. Before long he became Lt-Gen., commanding one of the two wings of the Army of Northern Virginia. His international fame continued to grow from his actions at 2nd Manassas, Fredericksburg, and Chancellorsville.

In Washington DC, federal leaders realized a successful invasion was much more complex than initially thought. As history repeatedly shows, the will of a people to defend themselves often proves more decisive than any military weaponry or invading army. Undoubtedly, the Confederates shocked the globe and confirmed they were more than farmers, led by skilled military leaders seeking to protect their homes. While much of Stonewall's focus was on defending and recapturing Winchester, Virginia, he wrote of his faith and hope for the future: "My little army is in excellent spirits. It feels that it inflicted a severe blow upon the enemy,"[298] adding, "After God, our God, again blesses us with peace, I hope to visit this country with my darling, and enjoy its beauty and loveliness."[299] R. L. Dabney disclosed a portion of a letter to Anna on March 24, 1862: "Our God was my shield. His protecting care is an additional cause for gratitude."[300]

Jackson's continued acknowledgment of God's protective care is evident in these following letters to Anna:

> April 7th 1862: Yesterday was a lovely Sabbath day. Although I had not the privilege of hearing the word of life, yet it felt like a holy Sabbath day, beautiful, serene and lovely. All it wanted was the church-bell and God's services in the sanctuary to make it complete. Our gallant little army is increasing in numbers, and my prayer is that it may be an army of the living God as well of its country.
>
> April 11th 1862: How precious is the consolation flowing from the Christian's assurance that all things work together for good to them that love God! God gave us a glorious victory in the Southwest (at Shiloh), but the loss of the great Albert Sidney Johnston is to be mourned. I do not remember having ever felt so sad at the death of a man whom I had never seen.[301]

Jackson knew that God provided for his army and protected his men. Knowing that he was never guaranteed survival in the temporary world, he remained confident that the Lord's hand guided all affairs by divine providence. Presbyterian William S. Plumer explained this internal comfort: "The righteous [believers]. They are safe, come what will. God, even the Father of our Lord Jesus Christ, has blessed them with all spiritual blessings in heavenly places in Christ Jesus. They are secured against all perils. They are sure of all mercies. Nothing shall ruin, nothing shall damage them. The everlasting God is their exceeding great reward and their unfailing portion."[302]

WCF 18.4 also teaches of such assurance:

> True believers may have the assurance of their salvation divers ways shaken, diminished, and intermitted; as, by negligence in preserving of it, by

falling into some special sin which woundeth the conscience and grieveth the Spirit; by some sudden or vehement temptation, by God's withdrawing the light of his countenance, and suffering even such as fear him to walk in darkness and to have no light: yet are they never utterly destitute of that seed of God, and life of faith, that love of Christ and the brethren, that sincerity of heart, and conscience of duty, out of which, by the operation of the Spirit, this assurance may, in due time, be revived; and by the which, in the meantime, they are supported from utter despair.[303]

Faith in Christ promised eternal peace and assurance. Certainly, such sentiments provided a comfort to Jackson that unbelievers could not relate to. Paul taught such in Romans 5:1 when he wrote, "Therefore being justified by faith, we have peace with God through our Lord Jesus Christ."

Fortified by this faith, Jackson and his men performed additional attacks though they were unsuccessful at Kernstown. This small town in the Shenandoah Valley was where Jackson suffered his only defeat, showcasing his resilience. The Union was shocked by Jackson's aggressive techniques and decided to send additional troops, giving them a numerical advantage over the Confederates.

This stage of the conflict remained difficult for any married couple, as visitations were almost non-existent. Jackson stayed consistent in his desire for peace and wholeheartedly felt the war would end soon, especially if his people prayed for peace from Jesus Christ. In one retreat, Jackson wrote: "But I remember that God reigns and is over all! And I know that has not come upon us by accident. God has ordered and permitted it, and He has been better to us than all our fears. His angel has certainly encamped around our dwelling, and no harm has happened to us. It is really wonderful how we have been protected, while others have suffered so from their depredations."[304]

Jackson consistently declared that the Lord protected his army and his fate in battle—rightfully so, as there are several accounts of him escaping near-massacre or capture. In Jackson's view, he was able to escape death by the grace of God. Jackson felt peace that the Lord remained with him. Plumer wrote on such an assurance: "Under the shadow of God's wings His people are safe from all their adversaries. He stills the enemy and the avenger." "Thou hast been a shelter for me, and a strong tower from the enemy" (Ps. 16:7). "God can make our worst enemies to be at peace with us" (Prov. 16:7).[305]

Throughout the war, conflicts emerged within Jackson's spiritual life. One such issue that constantly arose was honoring the Sabbath and fulfilling duty to the country, which often called for action on the Lord's Day. Responding to concerns about attacks on a Sabbath day, Jackson replied to his wife: "I was greatly concerned too; but I felt it my duty to do it, in consideration of the ruinous effects that might result from postponing the battle until the next morning. So far as I can see, my course was a wise one; the best that I could do under the circumstances, though very distasteful to my feelings, and I hope and pray to our Heavenly Father, that I may never again be in circumstances as on that day."[306]

The battles of the Civil War required that Jackson partake in several Sabbath day attacks. However, the general always sought to honor it the best he could. The desire to observe the Sabbath never disappeared; it was a frequent topic in discussions among himself and other officers. In May 1862, Jackson provided half a day of rest to his unit, declaring: "I congratulate you on your recent victory at McDowell. I request you to unite with me this morning in Thanksgiving to Almighty God for thus having crowned your arms with success, and in praying that He will continue to lead you on from victory to victory, until our independence shall be established, and makes us that people whose God is the Lord. The chaplains will hold divine service at ten o'clock A.M. this day in their respective regiments."[307]

If soldiers served in Jackson's brigade, they knew well that the emphasis on duty focused on Jesus Christ. While Stonewall believed only the Lord could open the heart of an unsaved sinner and provide regeneration, he believed his duty was to glorify God in everything he did (Col. 3:23) and ensure his army respected the teachings of the Holy Scriptures. Soldiers under his command grew familiar with Jackson's worldview and expectations. Strategic planning focused on the will of God, and he always sought earnest, genuine prayer. Jackson wrote the following to a friend: "My plan is to put on as bold a front as possible, to use every means in my power to prevent his advance whilst our reorganization is going on. What I desire is to hold the country as far as practicable, until we are in a condition to advance; and then with God's blessing let us make thorough work of it."[308]

In May 1862, the Confederates, led by Stonewall Jackson, defeated Union forces at Winchester. The losses were significantly less for the South compared to the North. Again, Stonewall attributed the success to a providential God, who allowed such a victory. Historian George C. Rable shared his logic: "A sovereign God literally decreed victories and defeats, and whatever course the war took, it reflected the divine will."[309] Theologian James Henley Thornwell (1812-1862) taught on providence:

> In the calumniated doctrine of an universal Providence, extending to all events and to all things, the only depositary of real efficiency and power, we find the true explanation of an activity which is neither casual in its origin nor a dependent link in an endless chain. In God we live and move and have our being. Nature and our own minds present us with multifarious phenomena linked together as antecedent and consequent, but all are equally effects. Neither nature nor ourselves present us with an instance of a real cause. To Him that sitteth on the throne, and to Him alone, in its just and proper sense, belongs the prerogative of Power. He speaks and it is done. He commands and it stands fast.[310]

Jackson's view of providence remained supported and taught by the Reformed confessions, the Scriptures, and leading Presbyterian theologians of his time. WSC explains,

> Q. What are the decrees of God?
>
> A. The decrees of God are his eternal purpose, according to the counsel of his will, whereby, for his own glory, he hath foreordained whatsoever comes to pass.[311]

Jackson's men achieved subsequent battle victories at Cross Keys and Port Republic. Chaplain Rev. J. William Jones reported on one instance: "While the battle was raging and the bullets were flying, Jackson rode by, calm as if he were at home, but his head raised toward heaven, and his lips were moving, evidently in prayer. Meeting a chaplain near the front in the heat of a battle, the general said to him, 'The rear is your place, sir, now, and prayer your business.'"[312]

In another circumstance, R.L. Dabney described Jackson's devoted faith amid battle: "As soon as Jackson uttered his command, he drew up his horse, and dropping the reins upon his neck, raised both his hands toward the heavens while the fire of battle in his face changed into a look of reverential awe. Even while he prayed, the God of battles heard; or ever he had withdrawn his uplifted hands the bridge was gained, and the enemy's gun was captured."[313]

Though the attributes of fearlessness had previously been displayed in the Mexican-American War, the authentic peace of understanding from his faith in Christ was new. Jackson did not fear death or injury. His ability to remain calm impressed his fellow soldiers, and his dependence on prayer and its power, even during battle, was nothing short of remarkable. Theologian Charles Hodge commented on prayer:

> This Supreme Power is roused into action by prayer in a way analogous to that in which the energies of a man are called into action by the entreaties of his

fellow men. This is the doctrine of the Bible; it is perfectly consistent with reason and is confirmed by the whole history of the world, and especially of the Church. Moses by his prayer saved the Israelites from destruction; at the prayer of Samuel the Army of the Philistines was dispersed, Elias was a man subject to like passions as we are, and he prayed earnestly that it might not rain; and it rained not on the earth by the space of three years and six months."[314]

On June 14, Jackson penned, "Our God has again thrown his [sic] shield over me in the various apparent dangers to which I have been exposed. This evening we have religious services in the army for the purpose of rendering thanks to the Most High for the victories with which He has crowned our arms, and to offer earnest prayer that He will continue to give us success, until, through His divine blessing, our independence shall be established."[315] Jackson's prayer life separated him from others, even from many Christians of his day. One of the most impressive growths in his walk with Christ was that of his prayer life and focus on the importance of prayer. Biographer John Esten Cooke noted: "Prayer was like breathing with him—the normal condition of his being. Every morning he read his Bible and prayed; and the writer will not soon forget the picture drawn by one of his distinguished associates, who rode to his headquarters at daylight in November 1862, when the army was falling back to Fredericksburg from the Valley, and found him reading his Testament, quietly in his tent—an occupation which he only interrupted to describe, in manners of quiet simplicity, his intended movements to foil the enemy."[316]

The logic is simple: How could God be with an army if the people did not seek His will? Jackson knew that every battle, whether a success or loss, resulted from the divine plan of the Lord. He also took to heart the Scriptures, which commanded him to ask for the Lord's intervention (Matt. 7:7). Rev. John Richardson commented, "Those who were skeptical of the sincerity of other men's prayers seemed to feel that when Jackson knelt, the heavens came down, indeed into communion of earth."[317] While Jackson obeyed the Scriptures in seeking God's wisdom, will, and direction, he also knew that not every prayer is answered unless it remains the will of God. He felt comfort in God's will, persevering in any circumstance. Presbyterian W.B. Sprague (1795-1876) wrote, "In every thing that relates to the present life you are to cherish a due sense of dependence on God."[318] He later added, "Thus making God your refuge and strength, you will be enabled to forget the things that are behind and press forward; and your path will shine brighter and brighter unto the perfect day."[319] The impact Jackson had on his men carried into the war. In one instance, Jedediah Hotchkiss, Stonewall's topographer, recalled a sermon and Lord's Supper that Jackson attended: "It was a very impressive celebration of the Lord's Supper, in the woods, amid the din of camps hushed for a brief period to celebrate the Supper of the Prince of Peace. The General attended the meeting, humbly devout."[320]

In the hot summer months of late June to July 1862, Jackson had difficulties maintaining his battle success, leading some historians to question his leadership. In what is referred to as the "Seven Day Battles," Jackson's Army showed up late in assisting General Robert E. Lee and consistently underperformed in regular attacks. A confusion of orders separated Lee and Jackson. Further, some scholars note that Jackson remained hesitant in necessary attacks, leading to further disorganization and defeats. Military historian G. F. R. Henderson summed up the loss and uncharacteristic battle experiences of Jackson:

> Had Jackson been at hand the pressure would in all probability have been applied. The contagion of defeat soon spreads; and whatever reserves a flying enemy may possess, if they are entrenched, their resistance is seldom long protracted. More than all, when night has fallen on the field, and prevents all estimate of the strength of the attack, a resolute advance has peculiar chances of success. But when his advanced line halted, Jackson was not yet up; and before he arrived,

the impetus victory had died away; the Federal reserves were deployed in a strong position, and the opportunity had already passed.... Jackson himself, it is said, came near capture."[321]

While many works criticize Jackson, he would have only affirmed his fallen nature as a mere creature living in God's ultimate design. Jackson, a fallible human being, made questionable decisions just as any other leader did in warfare.

Amid the arduous battles, Jackson wrote to Anna, "I do trust that our God will soon bless us with an honorable peace and permit us to be together at home again in the enjoyment of domestic happiness."[322] The general longed for his wife and home. Writing to Anna, he said: "You must give fifty dollars for church purposes, and more should you be disposed. Keep an account of the amount, as we must give at least one tenth of our income. I would like very much to see my darling, but hope that God will enable me to remain at the post duty until, in His own good time, He blesses us with independence.[323]

Similar to earlier accounts, the discussion of slavery came up in one letter to a fellow officer. Writing to Captain Barringer, Jackson mentioned:

> Neither of us had any special concern for slavery, but both agreed that if the sword was once drawn, the South would have no alternative but to defend her homes and firesides, slavery and all. I myself see in this war, if the North triumph a dissolution of the bonds of all society. It is not alone the destruction of our property, but it is the prelude to anarchy, infidelity, and the ultimate loss of free responsible government on this continent. With these convictions, I always thought we ought to meet the Federal invaders on the outer verge of just right and defense, and raise at once the black flag, viz., "No quarter to the violators

of our homes and fire sides!" It would in the end have proved true humanity and mercy. The Bible is full of such wars, and it is the only policy that would bring the North to its senses.[324]

The writer acknowledges that such statements will promote the narrative that Jackson fought for slavery. This remains far from an accurate position, as he constantly sought peace and clarified that the defense of Virginia was the only reason he stayed in Confederate ranks. Nonetheless, Jackson mentioned the right to slavery, underlining his position on constitutional state rights. Jackson viewed his duty as the defense of Virginia and its people.

In July, Jackson found temporary residence with the Ewings, a fellow church family. When available, Jackson joined the family in prayer and family worship. Mr. Ewing recalled: "There was something very striking in his prayers. He did not pray to men, but to God. His tones were deep, solemn, tremulous. He seemed to realize that he was speaking to Heaven's King. I never heard anyone pray who seemed to be pervaded more fully by a spirit of self-abnegation. He seemed to feel more than any man I ever knew the anger of robbing God of the glory due for our success."[325]

In another letter to Anna, Jackson penned, "A number of officers are with me, but people keep coming to my tent though let me say no more. A Christian should never complain. The apostle Paul said, 'I glory in tribulations! What a bright example for others!'"[326] Various accounts emerged both during and after the war, and the humbleness of Jackson served as an example for many (Jas. 4:10). Such humility was apparent when his army became victorious in an August campaign after which he ordered "no cheering, shouting or celebrating."[327] Instead, the soldiers walked one by one, passing their general, simply taking their caps off and acknowledging Stonewall quietly.[328] Chaplain Jones shared another story from a writer: "General Jackson never enters a battle without invoking God's blessing and protection. The dependence of this strange man upon the Deity seems never to be absent from his mind and whatever he says or does, it is always prefaced, 'by God's blessing.'

'By God's blessing we have defeated the enemy' is his laconic and pious announcement of a victory. One of his officers said to him, 'Well, general, another candidate is waiting your attention.' 'So I observe,' was the quiet reply, 'and by God's blessing, he shall receive it to his full satisfaction.'"[329]

While Jackson could not ignore his duties as general and the realities of war, he knew well that his purpose in life, even in battle, centered on glorifying the Lord. WSC states,

> Q. What is the chief end of man?
>
> A. Man's chief end is to glorify God, and to enjoy him forever.[330]

His biblical worldview taught that the Lord provided every victory, while Jackson and his men merely played a role in the sovereign hand of his Creator. While this worldview might confuse many—even those within Jackson's company—theologians historically depicted it in Christian teachings. The Old Testament served as an example of such thought, constantly referring to enemies being "given to Israel" or alternatively describing the success of enemies of Israel at times of turmoil and disobedience to the Lord's ways.

Accounts written to both General Lee and Anna provide insight into the Battle of Cedar. Also known as Cedar Mountain, the Confederates outnumbered the Union troops by almost double. In this exchange, Jackson again achieved victory. Dabney shared some of Stonewall's thoughts: "I can hardly think of the fall of Brigadier-General C. S. Winder, without tearful eyes. Let us all unite more earnestly in imploring God's aid in fighting our battles for us. The thought that there are so many of God's people praying for His blessing upon the army, which, in His Providence is, with me, greatly strengthens me. If God be for us, who can be against us?"[331]

In the bloodiest conflict in US history, the constant battles affected all soldiers. Christians like Stonewall also remained challenged, though what differentiated him from others was that he centered on the fact that the world was only a temporary home filled with much pain and sorrow. His time on earth was a spiritual test, one of great importance that set him apart from others, and centered on a doctrine of beliefs that precisely called him to serve the Lord daily (Luke 9:23–24).

Further summer battles ensued, with an ultimate victory at the 2nd Battle of Manassas. Similar to other engagements, the Confederates found themselves outnumbered; however, they accomplished an impressive victory. Again, a common occurrence appears in the earlier part of the war; Union forces continually underperformed in large confrontations. On this achievement, Jackson reported: "We should in all things acknowledge the hand of Him who reigns in Heaven, and rules among the armies of men. In view of the arduous labors and great privations the troops were called to endure, and the isolated and perilous position which the command occupied, while engaged with greatly superior numbers of the enemy, we can but express the grateful conviction of our mind, that God was with us, and gave us the victory; and unto His holy name be the praise."[332]

Jackson would praise the Lord with triumph and yet praise the Lord in defeat. He knew that the providence of God Almighty assisted in several decisive victories. One officer remarked to Jackson, "General, this victory has been won by the determined valor of our soldiers, by plain, hard fighting."[333] Jackson responded, "Don't forget, it has been won by the help of God."[334] Understandably, Jackson felt he had the advantage in battle if his men lived for the Lord. He passionately taught his men, Providence dictated outcomes, including all victories.

In his October 6th letter to Anna, Stonewall wrote: "I am glad that you were privileged to keep Thanksgiving Day. We did not enjoy that blessing. I regret to say. I trust it was generally observed, and that rich blessings may flow from it through our ever-kind Heavenly Father. I also hope that on that day large contributions were made to our Bible society. You and I have, as you say, special reason for gratitude to God for His goodness and mercy to us."[335]

Historically, Thanksgiving played an important role in American culture and solely focused for many people, especially Christians, on providing gratitude to the Lord. An analysis of the holiday supports such a position, as it formed upon a thankfulness to God for allowing the original Pilgrims to survive the wrath of a harsh winter. Throughout the passing generations, the sole focus for many emphasized the connection to Christianity. While Thanksgiving was historically significant to all, Jackson knew the Christian's life called for daily thanksgiving and submission to God's will (Ps. 68:19).

The rest of the fall became pivotal in General Lee's strategic operations. Jackson became lieutenant general, being given the command of half of Lee's Army. The Union stumbled to understand battle outcomes on the other side of the conflict. Leadership changes continuously occurred in the North, with the Union realizing that defeating General Lee was proving much more complicated than initially anticipated.

In retelling a recent sermon within the camp, Jackson shared: "It was a powerful exposition of the Word of God; and when he (Rev. Stiles) came to the word *himself,* he placed an emphasis upon it, and gave it a force which I had never felt before, and I realized that, truly, the sinner who does not, under Gospel privileges, turn to God deserves the agonies of perdition. The doctor several times, in appealing to the sinner, repeated the 6th verse—"Who gave himself a ransom for all, to be testified in due time." What more could God do than to give himself a ransom?"[336]

Stonewall and Anna welcomed the birth of their daughter Julia Laura, named after Jackson's younger sister and mother. Jackson rejoiced in excitement upon learning of the birth, "Oh how thankful I am to our kind Heavenly Father for having spared my precious wife and given us a little daughter! I cannot tell you how gratified I am, nor how much I wish I could be with you, and see my two darlings."[337]

In December 1862, the Confederates, decisively defeated the Union at Fredericksburg. Days before the battle, Jackson wrote to Anna, "December 4th: Wherever I go, God gives me kind friends. The people here show me great kindness.[338]...I am so thankful to our ever-kind Heavenly Father for having so improved my eyes as to enable me to write at night. He continually showers blessings upon me; and that you should have been spared, and our darling daughter given us, fills my heart with overflowing gratitude. If I know my unworthy self, my desire is to live entirely and unreservedly to God's glory. Pray, my darling, that I may so live."[339] Anna recounted another fascinating story that came on the eve of the battle: "A chaplain saw an officer wrapped in his overcoat so that his marks of rank could not be seen, lying just in the rear of a battery, quietly reading his Bible. He approached and entered into conversation on the prospects of the impending battle, but the officer soon changed the conversation to religious topics, and the chaplain led to ask, 'Of what regiment are you a chaplain?' What was his astonishment to find that the quiet Bible-reader and fluent talker upon religious subjects was none other than the famous Stonewall Jackson."[340]

This battle-worn soldier was devoted to prayer and contemplated the Scriptures. Jackson knew the importance of time with God and personal devotion to the Lord. On desiring more knowledge of Christ, the great theologian Archibald Alexander (1812-1851) penned, "Christians are compared to 'new-born-babes,' who naturally thirst for the pure milk of the word, that they may grow thereby. Their growth depends very much on their increased knowledge; the word of God, therefore, is the means of the believer's advancement in the divine life."[341]

After the Battle of Fredericksburg, the casualties were exceptionally high for the Union Army, which lost over twelve-thousand troops. Jackson therefore believed that his army maintained the heavenly blessings from above. Consistent victories occurred, often overachieving even the standards of their own ranks. Jackson knew his success remained at the providential will of the Lord. Submission to the Lord's will mattered more to Jackson than any battle win or loss. Dabney recalled one instance where Jackson appealed to a friend who was not a follower of Christ: "Nothing earthly can mar my happiness. I know that heaven is in store for me; and I should rejoice in the prospect of going there tomorrow. Understand me: I am not sick; I am not sad; God has greatly blessed me; and I have as much to love here as any man, and life is very bright to me. But, still, I am ready to leave it any day, without trepidation or regret, for that heaven which I know awaits me, through the mercy of my Heavenly Father."[342]

Passionately, Jackson summed up his reliance on the Lord with such a quote. Despite astonishing victories on the battlefield, the assurance of living for God and submitting to His glory gave him confidence that no other could possess outside of Christ. What Jackson indicated in such a statement supported his understanding of saving faith as conveyed in WCF 14.2:

> By this faith, a Christian believeth to be true whatsoever is revealed in the Word, for the authority of God himself speaking therein; and acteth differently upon that which each particular passage thereof containeth; yielding obedience to the commands, trembling at the threatenings, and embracing the promises of God for this life, and that which is to come. But the principal acts of saving faith are accepting, receiving, and resting upon Christ alone for justification, sanctification, and eternal life, by virtue of the covenant of grace.[343]

In a similar declaration outlining the importance of observing the Sabbath, like during the years before, Jackson urged the Confederacy leadership to honor this holy day:

> I do not see how a nation that thus arrays itself, by such a law, against God's holy day, can expect to escape His wrath.... I have never sustained loss in observing what God enjoins; and I am well satisfied that the law should be repealed at the earliest practicable moment. My rule is, to let the Sabbath mails remain unopened, unless they contain a dispatch; but dispatches are generally sent by couriers or telegraph, or some special messenger.... I understand that not only

our President (Davis), but also most of his Cabinet, and a majority of our Congressmen, are professing Christians. God has greatly blessed us, and I trust He will make us that people whose God is the Lord. Let us look to God for an illustration in our history, that righteousness exalteth a nation, but sin is a reproach to any people.[344]

Interestingly, the fact that mail continued to be delivered and distributed on the Sabbath notably bothered Jackson. However, the concern centered on abiding by the Lord's commandments. Accordingly, he questioned how a nation could expect the blessing of the Lord if it denied His Word and commandments (John 14:15, 21). This reasoning was not new, and devout Christians preceding Jackson argued the same principle. A nation that followed the Lord Jesus Christ could expect His blessings; however, those who openly denied His ways needed to be prepared for judgment. Such a possibility troubled Jackson, primarily when engaged in such a bloody conflict where the Lord's guidance was so desperately needed. Summing up the campaign of 1862, Jackson's staff officer, Henry Kyd Douglas wrote: "History can never know the whole truth. The historian may analyze, investigate, and speculate until he is weary, and knowing the small and uncertain means with which such great results were achieved, he may pronounce it all wonderful; yet his conclusion will fall short of the truth. General Jackson seldom, if ever, complained, and never uselessly and apologetically to those under him, nor to those above him. Determined to deserve good fortune, he never quailed before disaster; but trusting God, himself and his army he always commanded success."[345]

1863

Stonewall had great spiritual concern for the entire Confederate Army. Like General Lee, he sought every opportunity to implement the Christian doctrine and standards of the faith. Chaplain White tells one story of Jackson's prayers and how they assisted in his fellow officer's conversion to the faith:

> I have it from a well-authenticated source that the conversion of Lieutenant-General Ewell, Jackson's able lieutenant, was on this wise: At a council of war, one night, Jackson had listened very attentively to the views of his subordinates and asked until the next morning to present his own. As they came away, A. P. Hill laughingly said to Ewell, "Well I suppose Jackson wants time to pray over it." Having the occasion to return to his quarters again a short time after, Ewell found Jackson on his knees and heard his ejaculatory prayers for God's guidance in the perplexing movements then before him. The sturdy veteran was so deeply impressed by this incident and by Jackson's general religious character, that he said, "If that is religion, I must have it."[346]

Here Jackson's faithfulness resembled that of David (Ps. 25), as he sought the Lord's guidance, deliverance, and will. More impressively, the Lord Jesus taught such an example, praying for God's will, "Father, if you are willing, take this cup from me; yet not my will, but yours be done." (Luke 22:42)

In another situation, Henry Kyd Douglas recounted, "At the close of the Battle of Republic, he [Jackson] rode to General Ewell and laying his hand gently on his arm and said, 'General, he who does not see the hand of God in this is blind, Sir, blind!'"[347] Dick Taylor who served with Jackson and Ewell recalled, "He sucked lemons, ate hard tack, and drank water, and praying and fighting appeared to be his idea of the whole duty of man."[348] Charles L. Dufour further recounts Taylor's view on Jackson: "I have written that he was ambitious; and his ambition was vast, all-absorbing. Like the unhappy wretch from who shoulders sprang the foul serpent, he loathed it, perhaps feared it; but he could not escape it—it was himself—nor rend it—it was his own flesh. He fought it with prayer, constant and earnest—Apollyon and Christian in ceaseless combat. What limit to set to his ability I know not, for he was ever superior to the occasion."[349]

In another letter, Jackson wrote:

> My views are summed up in these few words. Each Christian branch of the Church should send into the army some of its most prominent ministers, who are distinguished for their piety, talents, and zeal; and such ministers should labor to produce concert of action among chaplains and Christians in the army. These ministers should give special attention to preaching to regiments which are without chaplains and induce them to take steps to get chaplains; to let the regiments name the denominations from which they desire chaplains selected; and then to see that suitable chaplains are secured. If a few prominent ministers thus connected with each army would cordially co-operate, I believe the glorious fruits would be the results.... I would like to see no questions asked in the army as to what denomination a chaplain belongs; but let the question be, "Does he preach the Gospel?" The neglect of spiritual interests in the army may be partially seen in the fact that not half of my regiments have chaplains.[350]

Jackson differentiated genuine Christianity from nominal Christianity. It is easy to be a professing Christian, but much harder and personal to be a follower who surrenders to the Lord's will. The standards were relatively simple: Did chaplains preach the Gospel and rely on the Scriptures as their ultimate authority? If so, Stonewall felt confident about their service in the field. The Westminster Confession supported his view on the authority of the Bible:

> The authority of the Holy Scripture, for which it ought to be believed, and obeyed, dependeth not upon the

testimony of any man, or church; but wholly upon God (who is truth itself) the author thereof: and therefore it is to be received, because it is the Word of God. (WCF 1.4) [351]

And Jackson proudly defended and argued for his Presbyterian faith, he acknowledged the concept of the invisible church, being one body in Christ:

> The catholic or universal church, which is invisible, consists of the whole number of the elect, that have been, are, or shall be gathered into one, under Christ the Head thereof; and is the spouse, the body, the fullness of him that filleth all in all. (WCF 25.1)[352]

Sadly, on both sides of the war, the teaching of liberal universalism was prominent. In short, this teaching argued that Jesus Christ died for all humanity, even those who never experienced spiritual regeneration. Jackson believed that universalism was not only bad theology, but also dangerous as it led people astray from the Scriptures and towards eternal damnation. Salvation could only be achieved through Jesus Christ.

While Jackson's fame grew worldwide, his nephew, Thomas, mentioned that in England especially, great admiration appeared. Arnold reported, "Jackson in the latter part of his life only read two books, the Bible and the campaigns of Napoleon."[353] In his book on Southern Presbyterians, Henry Alexander White commented, "Jackson was afterwards revealed to the world as a great military genius, Stonewall Jackson; it was at the same time made clear to all who knew him that he was a man of faith and of prayer. His nature was saturated with the Biblical idea of life. He had an intense sense of God's presence with him. In every incident of life, he saw the visible finger of God, and every victory that he won was ascribed to Providence."[354]

During and after the war, European generals studied the American Civil War. They often acknowledged that some of the most brilliant campaigns fought in the world's history took place within this deadly confrontation. Rev. John R. Richardson wrote, "It has been stated that Marshal Rommel [German General WWII] studied the campaigns of Stonewall Jackson very carefully and employed its strategy during his first campaigns in Africa."[355]

In 1863, Jackson's fame continued, as did his success. He pursued the enemy and played an integral part in various victories. Jackson became a reliable hand for General Lee, and the two grew stronger as allies and close confidants. His former brigade, too, grew in acclamation, often referred to by others as a brigade of Christian conviction. In one post-battle speech, Jackson declared, "But his chief duty today, and that of the army, is to recognize devoutly the hand of a protecting Providence in the brilliant successes of the last three days; and to make the oblation of our thanks to God for his mercies to us and our country, in heartfelt acts of religious worship."[356] Henry Kyd Douglas recalled an instance in a battle where a fellow soldier proclaimed, "Old Jack got us into this fix, and with the blessing of God he will get us out."[357]

Jackson penned to Anna in February 1863: "I trust, that in answer to the prayers of God's people, He will soon give us peace. I haven't seen my wife for nearly a year, and my home for nearly two years; and I never have seen my sweet little daughter. My old brigade has built a log church; as yet I have not been in it."[358]

Jackson earnestly sought peace for his nation. He felt confident that peace could come through prayer, thankfulness, praise, and submission to God's will. He wrote to Colonel Preston,

> I greatly desire to see Peace, blessed peace.... Let our Government acknowledge the God of the Bible as its God, and we may expect soon to be a happy and independent people. It appears to me that the extremes are to be avoided; and it also appears to me that the old United States occupied an extreme position in the

means it took to prevent the Union of Church and State. We call ourselves a Christian people; and it seems to me that our Government may be of the same character, without connecting itself with an established church. It does appear to me that our President, our Congress, and our people have thanked God for victories, and prayed to Him for additional ones, and He has answered such prayers, and gives us a Government, [*sic*] it is gross ingratitude not to acknowledge Him in the gift. Let the framework of our Government show that we are not ungrateful to Him.[359]

While perhaps prematurely, Jackson desired a permanent nation known as the Confederate States of America. Within this government, he argued that the foundation of the system needed to rely on the Lord Himself, including adherence to the Holy Scriptures. Plumer taught on God's providence within the nations, "God claims to be the Father and Founder of the nations,"[360] adding, "God has often threatened to punish nations, to be avenged on them, yea, to cast into hell the nations that forget God."[361] While the United States remained influenced by Christianity, it was never—and currently is not—a Christian nation. The separation of Church and State makes this abundantly clear. Though Jackson knew the government, and even he himself, could not forcibly convert souls to Christ, it was still his prayer and desire to form a government solely focused on God found in the Scriptures. The preamble of the Confederate Constitution, unlike that of the U.S., called for God's blessing.

Jackson's brilliance grew and assisted the Confederates in many minor skirmishes and great battle victories. We can also find plenty of books on the Confederate Army's spiritual revival. Jackson emphasized the importance of surrendering all aspects of life, including battle logistics, to the will of God. Dabney believed that there had not been such a revival since George Whitefield's days. Wherever Jackson's tent lay, great chaplains preached sermons. With the attendance continually growing in numbers, Dabney recalled, "From hundreds it grew to thousands, until the assemblage surrounded the preacher in a compact mass, as far as his voice could be distinctly heard."[362] Prayers such as the following were often heard:

> O GOD, we beseech Thee, forgive and pardon our enemies, and give us that measure of Thy grace, that for their hatred we may love them; for their cursing we may bless them; for their injury we may do them good; and for their persecution we may pray for them. They have laid a net for our steps, and they have digged a pit before us; Lord, we desire not that they themselves should fall into the midst of these, but we beseech Thee keep us out of them, and deliver, establish, bless and prosper us for Thy mercy's sake in Jesus Christ our Saviour, to whom with Thee and the Holy Spirit, we desire to consecrate ourselves and our country, now and forever, imploring Thee to be our God, and to make us Thy people. Amen.[363]

Henry Kyd Douglas recalled one particular prayer meeting: "Bowed heads, bent knees, hats off, silence! Stonewall Jackson was kneeling to the Lord of Hosts, in prayer for his people! Not a sound disturbed his voice, as it ascended to Heaven in their behalf and, in their faith, the very stars seemed to move softly and make no noise. When he left, a line of soldiers followed him in escort to the edge of the camp, and then, doubtless, returned to their cards. From a scene like this one, made vivid by the pencil of Vizetelly, came, I fancy, the engraving, 'Prayer in Stonewall Jackson's Camp.'"[364]

On the Confederate side, something extraordinary occurred. Within much of the army, a sense of understanding prevailed. Not every soldier became a follower of Christ, but the impact that Jackson and other Christian military leaders had on the soldiers continued for the remainder of the war.

The Death of Stonewall Jackson

The engagement at Chancellorsville was a massive collision of forces that resulted in devastating casualties for both sides, though the Confederates, by all accounts, achieved victory. The Union forces neared one-hundred-thousand troops and vastly outnumbered the Confederates. In this particular bloody campaign, Jackson's reputation held strong, as he displayed his courageous, brilliant skills. Chaplain Jones recalled meeting Jackson days before the battle: "Upon one occasion, I called at Jackson's headquarters and found him just going in to a prayer meeting which he was accustomed to hold. I gladly accepted his invitation to attend, and shall never forget the power, comprehensiveness, and tender pathos of the prayer he made during that delightful prayer meeting."[365]

The day of the battle, as dark was descending, Jackson was shot by Confederate soldiers in an accident of friendly fire. Two units came into contact suddenly and mistook Jackson's men as Union forces. In the confusion of a surprise attack by his own men, Jackson suffered gravely, being hit several times. John Esten Cooke reported:

> He had not gone twenty steps into the woods when a Confederate brigade, which was there drawn up within twenty yards of him, delivered a volley in their turn, kneeling on the right knee, as the flash of the guns showed, as though preparing to guard against cavalry. By this fire Jackson was wounded in three places. He received one ball in his left arm, two inches below the shoulder joint, shattering the bone and severing the chief artery; a second passed through the same arm, between the elbow and wrist, making its exit through the palm of the hand; and a third ball entered the palm of his right hand, about the middle, and passing through, broke two of the bones.[366]

While hit by his men, the Union troops were only a "hundred yards away." [367] Several of the soldiers with Jackson died instantly, and the general remained gravely injured. Jackson's last official orders exclaimed, "General Pender, you must hold on the field; you must hold out last."[368] The situation became clear that men had just fired upon their own army, and the threat remained with Union troops led by scouts made their way into the vicinity, even close to killing Jackson, who laid on the ground wounded.

Rushing through the woods, soldiers carrying him dropped him several times as constant fire continued, even striking down a soldier who was carrying him.[369] Of course, such injuries resulted in his condition going from bad to worse. Those surviving moved urgently to get Jackson to safety as he quietly asked for a surgeon. Jackson knew he was severely wounded and needed help badly. He said that he thought he was dying.[370] Surprisingly, losing much blood and going in and out of consciousness, he made it to a camp. Once the attendants knew who lay hurt, several doctors rushed to treat the general. Jackson lived several days, some even thinking he might end up healing. During his remaining days, Jackson conversed with doctors, chaplains, and fellow soldiers. Anna recorded some comments from one of those doctors, Dr. McGuire: "The men of the brigade will be, some day, proud to say to their children, 'I was one of *The Stonewall Brigade.*' Jackson responded, 'It (title) belongs to the brigade, and not to me, for it was their steadfast heroism which earned it at First Manassas.'"[371]

Jackson required amputation of his limb. This shockingly successful operation provided some hope to the doctor. After the operation, Jackson remarked to Chaplain Beverly Tucker Lacy:

> You see me severely wounded, but not depressed, not unhappy. I believe it has been done according to God's holy will, and I acquiesce entirely in it. You may think it strange, but you never saw me more perfectly contented than I am today; for I am sure that my Heavenly Father designs affliction for my good. I am perfectly satisfied that, either in this life, or in that which is to come, I shall discover that what

is now regarded as a calamity is a blessing. And if it appears a great calamity, as it surely will be a great inconvenience, to be deprived of my arm, it will result in a great blessing. I can wait until God, in His own time, shall make known to be the object He has in thus afflicting me. But why should I not rather rejoice in it as a blessing, and not look on it as a calamity at all? If it were in my power to replace my arm, I would not dare to do it, unless I could know it was the will of my Heavenly Father.[372]

Impressed with Jackson's submission to God, Lacy took notes of the encounter, later sharing the general's words with other chaplains. Jackson genuinely felt his time on earth had not ended, and he told those around him that he felt confident he was not dying. Of course, from his admission, if the Lord desired his time to come, he remained prepared to accept such a fate.

Interestingly, his military interest in the current situation at Chancellorsville continued. Speaking of battle specifics, he even brought in the Bible, "Look, for instance, at the narrative of Joshua's battle with the Amalekites; there you have one. It has clearness, brevity, fairness, modesty; and it traces the victory to its right source, the blessing of God."[373] Chancellorsville lasted several days, during which soldiers constantly reminded Jackson that his military brilliance assisted in the ultimate victory. Even while lying sick in bed, Jackson gave all glory to God: "Our movement yesterday was a great success; I think the most successful military movement of my life. But I expect to receive far more credit for it than I deserve. Most men will think I had planned it all from the first; but it was not so—I simply took advantage of circumstances as they were presented to me in the Providence of God. I feel that His hand led me: let us give Him all the glory."[374]

Jackson was slowly slipping away from thromboembolism, the consequences of his wounds and amputation, along with pneumonia. He also fought a consistent fever that started changing his attitude and demeanor. His doctors believed that the severe falls from soldiers dropping him played an especially vital role in further damage. Those working on him all felt confident that Jackson was dying. Thankfully, his wife Anna made her way to see him. From one eyewitness account, "Jackson said to her (Anna), 'I know you would gladly give your life for me, but I am perfectly resigned. Do not be sad. I hope I may yet recover.' Pray for me, but always remember in your prayers to use the petition, 'Thy will be done.'"[375]

It remains essential to hear from Anna:

> When I told him the doctors thought he would soon be in heaven, he did not seem to comprehend it, and showed no surprise, or concern. But upon repeating it and asking him if he was willing for God to do with him according to His own will, he looked at me calmly and intelligently, and said, "Yes, I prefer it, I prefer it." I then told him that before that day was over he would be with the blessed Saviour in His glory. With perfect distinctness and intelligence, he said, "I will be an infinite gainer to be translated."…I then asked him if it was his wish that I should return, with our infant, to my father's home in North Carolina. He answered, "Yes, you have a kind, good father, but no one is so kind and good as your Heavenly Father."[376]

At this time, Jackson became incoherent. Most of his statements appeared to be military orders. Thankfully, his baby daughter, Julia, too, came into his presence before his passing, to whom he remarked, "Little darling! Sweet one!"[377] The general's last words exclaimed, "Let us cross over the river, and rest under the shade of trees."[378] Some scholars think this referenced his time on Uncle Cummins' homestead with his sister, Laura. Others remain adamant it was a military order. And some acclaim it was the ultimate feeling of his soul passing into the Lord's presence. Whatever the phrase meant, Jackson died peacefully, being received into his Savior's glory.

Chaplain Jones recalls his death, "In fine, [sic] Jackson took Jesus as his Saviour, his Guide, his great Exemplar, 'the Captain of his salvation,' whom he followed with unquestioning obedience of the true soldier. And having thus lived, it is not surprising that he died the glorious death which has been described."[379] Displaying the submission to God's will on death, Jackson served as a prime example of one surrendering his life to the Lord. Plumer wrote on death: "The last enemy that shall be destroyed is death (1 Corinthians 15:26). He has tyrannized over the world for a long time, and his power will be more or less felt till death and hell shall be cast into the lake of fire. Therefore, he shall have no power even to mar the bliss of the saints. Mighty is the power and wondrous is the grace of him who can destroy the tyrant who for centuries has gone forth conquering and prostrating before him one generation after another. Blessed be God for Jesus Christ."[380] WSC plainly states:

> Q. What benefits do believers receive from Christ at death?
>
> A. The souls of believers are at their death made perfect in holiness, and do immediately pass into glory; and their bodies, being still united to Christ, do rest in their graves till the resurrection.[381]

General Robert E. Lee announced the death of Jackson to the soldiers:

> With deep grief, the commanding general announces to the army the death of Lieutenant-General T.J. Jackson, who expired on the 10th inst., at a quarter past 3 P.M. The daring, skill and energy of this great and good soldier are now, by the decrees of an all-wise Providence, lost to us. But while we mourn his death, we feel that his spirit still lives, and will inspire the whole army with his indomitable courage and unshaken confidence in God as our help and strength. Let his name be a watchword to his corps, who have followed

him to victory on so many fields. Let his officers and soldiers emulate his invincible determination to do everything in the defense of our beloved country.[382]

While many noble soldiers, including generals, had died, Lee knew replacing Jackson was impossible. No replacement could match his brilliance, fearlessness, and dependence on the Lord in battle. Jackson's remains were buried in Lexington upon his death, and the war continued.

Chaplain White shared the legacy of Jackson, from a story of one child who attended his African-American Sabbath School: "The Federal Army was occupying the town (Lexington), bearing fresh flowers with which to decorate the hero's grave, (a townswoman) was surprised to find a miniature Confederate flag planted on the grave with a verse of a familiar hymn pinned to it. Upon inquiry she found that a colored boy, who had belonged to Jackson's Sunday-school, had procured the flag, gotten someone to copy a stanza of a favorite hymn which Jackson had taught him, and had gone in the night to plant the flag on the grave of his loved teacher."[383]

Jackson's priority was to be remembered for his faith in Jesus Christ, not his military accomplishments. His faith assisted several in conversions:

> It is impossible to exaggerate the influence that Stonewall Jackson exerted upon the men in the Confederate Army. Mr. W.P. St. John, president of the Mercantile Bank of New York relates this incident. He stated that he was in the Shenandoah Valley with Gen. Thomas Jordan and at the close of the day, they found themselves at the foot of the mountains in a wild and lonely place. The only place they could find for rest was a rough shanty. There they found a rough looking, unshaven man. They were amazed when the time came to eat that this rough backwoodsman rapped on the table and bowed his head and prayed. The banker

said, "Never did I hear a petition that more evidently came from the heart. It was so simple, so reverent, so tender, so full of humility, and penitence, as well as thankfulness. We sat in silence and as soon as we recovered, I whispered to Gen. Jordan, 'Who can he be?' To which he answered, 'I don't know, but he must be one of Stonewall Jackson's old soldiers.' And he was." They asked him, "Were you in the war?" "Oh, yes," he said with a smile, "I was with old Stonewall."[384]

Dabney remarked on the legacy of Jackson:

> He makes all men see and acknowledge that in this man Christianity was the source of those virtues which they so rapturously applauded; that it was the fear of God which made him so fearless of all else; that it was the love of God which animated his energies; that it was the singleness of his aims which caused his whole body to be full of light; so that the unerring decision of his judgment suggested to the unthinking the belief of his actual inspiration; that the lofty chivalry of his nature was but the reflex of the spirit of Christ.[385]

The words of John Esten Cooke best challenge our soul:

> Napoleon trusted in his star—Jackson in God. Napoleon was a pure and simple fatalist. Jackson's motto was, "Do your duty, and leave the rest to Providence." One was a great soldier of imperial genius—but no more. The other was a mighty leader, but a humble, faithful child of God, as well. He accepted the lot decreed him by the Almighty Father with submission and humble hope, believing that whatever God permitted was the best. Let us, too, trust that all is well and look beyond the storm—beyond the darkness, blood, and

mourning of the present—with serene trust in Him who rules the destinies of men and nations.[386]

Conclusion

Jackson died at age thirty-nine. The man accomplished much in such a short time, including finding himself in the history books as one of the most strategically impressive military leaders of any generation. The campaigns in which he fought during the years of 1862 and 1863 proved that his leadership played an essential role in Confederate victories. Though if you would have asked Jackson, it was not his own doing, but the steady hand of his Lord and Savior guiding and providing him victories. However, it was not the victories he desired; he sought peace. He prayed for peace; he asked others to pray for peace and wanted an end to the conflict. Jackson longed for home and to be with his wife and his newborn child though, in his own words, he could not guarantee that outcome and would surrender to the will of God, even if it meant a departure from his temporary home on earth. The latter remained his fate.

Jackson died peacefully, submitting to the will of Jesus Christ. Peace eventually came, though with continued bloodshed and thousands losing their lives. While Jackson excelled in warfare and perhaps even enjoyed it in his younger years, the general cared more for his Savior than anything else. The challenge and desire of Jackson remain. What would a nation look like if its people followed the Lord Jesus Christ? How would it be possible for an army or enemy to defeat a country following the King? This was perhaps but a dream for Jackson, as it is today, but the reader is left contemplating the challenges of Jackson and asking themselves if they resemble the famed military leader in prayer, faithfulness, obedience, and the desire to glorify the Lord in their daily lives. May we pray that we build the life and legacy of Stonewall Jackson upon the regeneration of souls versus the admiration of his military might, as this would be his desire.

Conclusion

HURT, PAIN, SUFFERING, trials, and tribulations might describe the life of Stonewall Jackson; however, the author maintains that Stonewall would never have submitted to such characterizations. Stonewall viewed himself as a child of God, one saved by the grace of the Lord Jesus Christ. While the reader might feel deep sympathy and broken-heartedness when studying Jackson's life and sudden death, he surrendered to the will of his Lord and Savior and knew it meant all things for the good according to his sovereign Creator's plan. Can we say the same today? Have we entirely submitted to the providence of God Almighty? Do we seek Him daily, studying Him and His will in our lives?

Jackson undoubtedly experienced a tough childhood. Thankfully, his mother's influence on his life never disappeared, nor did her prayers go unanswered as the Lord called Stonewall to become a believer himself. While, by all accounts, the man who made the most significant impact on his childhood, Uncle Cummins, was not in the faith, he nevertheless reared Stonewall up in a respectable and honorable fashion. The Christian must acknowledge today that the Lord's providence often uses those, too, outside of the faith, to fulfill His will on earth. The Bible is full of such examples, from Moses being raised by an Egyptian pagan woman to Daniel remaining a faithful servant to various leaders from a variety of faiths. The Lord's hand was assured in Jackson's upbringing, and His sovereign will endured.

Stonewall Jackson: Saved By Providence

Jackson's childhood made him a tough, brave, and independent person. It takes a long time for many to understand their true calling in life. The Lord directed Jackson in his future and made it clear he was to become a military man: a fierce, brave soldier with unique traits that continue to be studied today. From his education at West Point to his service in the Mexican-American War, Jackson impressed many, and the Lord began his legacy. While perhaps not the most exciting or preferred professor, we affirm that the students who learned under Jackson gained wisdom and instruction, traits that were of the most benefit to them in the upcoming Civil War. The same students who complained about Jackson as a dry, boring, and strict professor soon served and died for him on the battlefield. And many would claim it was their greatest honor to serve under Jackson, whom most considered a faithful Christian, before any noble title of a military leader. One earns a legacy; it is never freely given. The Lord was gracious with Jackson, allowing him to impact countless soldiers and souls.

It does not take long to compare the life of Jackson to several biblical figures. Jackson maintained the bravery, courage, and faithfulness of Joshua. The Lord blessed him with the faith and leadership of King David. He had the inner strength and battle abilities of Samson and the wisdom of Solomon. And perhaps most telling, he possessed the humility and humbleness of Joseph. The reader should marvel at the Christian witness and testimony of Stonewall Jackson when studying his life and faith in Jesus Christ. Remember that he would point you only to the Lord Jesus Christ. And all can agree that it was faith in Christ and the work of the Holy Spirit that transformed this man into a faithful Christian.

While military service was his vocation, Jackson also married twice, learning from each marriage and growing from each bond. The Lord ordained his future and enabled both Ellie and Anna to further strengthen, test, and develop Jackson's Christian spirit. His calling was simple: to glorify and love the Lord with all of his heart, soul, and mind. The man was not perfect; he had his flaws as we all do, but Stonewall Jackson serves as a Christian example even today.

Conclusion

Imagine a world in which more people maintain the faith of the late general and surrender their own lives to the will of God.

While most people recall the military exploits of the Civil War as his legacy, he would have preferred to be known as a Christian. He did not seek war, but peace. His last letters affirm such a position; he longed to return to his wife, Anna, his daughter, and home. The man who perhaps embraced—and almost loved—warfare desired peace and love within the context of a Christian home and land. The reader must never forget that Jackson earnestly desired Christianity in all forms, from within his own life, house, family, land, and army. How did this once war-minded, brilliant leader mellow and prefer the way of Christ? The answer is simple: through faith in Jesus Christ. If you seek understanding, peace, knowledge, and wisdom, you can find it only in salvation through Jesus Christ.

Imagine a Christian Army, utterly full of believers of Jesus Christ, submitting to His will and seeking to bring forth the salt and light of the Earth. This was Jackson's dream. Such sentiments seem familiar to that of Joshua. Like Joshua, Jackson desired first for his family to serve the Lord (Josh. 24:15). The readers know that Jackson's dream was, and is not, a reality in this fallen world—at least not yet. But rest assured, Jackson is in glory, spending eternity with his Lord and Savior. And never forget, the Lord is returning, and with His next return, the world will tremble at His power and majesty.

If Jackson were alive today, he would ask, "Where are you spending eternity? Are you seeking the sin and enjoyment of the temporary but dark world, or are you living faithfully with the Lord and Savior Jesus Christ?" Really, little has changed, as our sin covers the world in darkness, and Jesus is not the center of any land or nation. If the reader gains one appreciation from this study, the prayer is that you focus on the saving power of Jesus Christ. You, too, can be like Stonewall Jackson, walking with Jesus Christ in daily affairs. You, too, can love, trust, submit to, and obey Christ. Place your faith in Christ and allow Him to do wonders in your life.

Stonewall Jackson died in a similar way to his mother: submitting to the will of God. Understandably, he wondered if he might survive, but he did not. The Lord called him home, and he shared with Anna, "I prefer it." We, too, would prefer being with the Lord Christ, in the Heaven of no tears or sorrow (Rev. 21:4). In the bloodiest conflict in US history, Jackson experienced his fair share of loss and tragic destruction, a common trait in his life, perhaps similar to yours. Jackson suffered severe, devastating injuries, and the General no longer needed to suffer in his temporary home. He did not fight death or curse God in anger. He submissively surrendered to the will of God and carried on into Glory. May the Lord grant us the patience and submission of the general.

Jackson was human, filled with sin like you and me, but he proved that with faithfulness in Christ alone, we can overcome Satan and the power of darkness over this world. As he so eloquently taught, you have two options. One is living in carnal sin and eventually dying; the other is living in faith and submission to the Lord Jesus Christ and eventually dying. Which one will lead you to Heaven? The Scriptures are clear: Only faith in Jesus Christ saves. And the one who places faith in Christ obeys Him, loves Him, and lives for Him. Are you willing to surrender everything in your life for the sake of Christ, including your own life? Then be like Stonewall Jackson and follow Christ.

Do you pray and live in thanksgiving? Do you thank the Lord for every sip of water you take or seek individual peace and devotion to the Lord? Amid battle, what did Stonewall do? He urged his chaplains to pray, looked to the heavens, and sought to fulfill the Lord's will. Before and after battles, soldiers found him praying and studying the Scriptures. The life of Stonewall Jackson centered on his prayer life, and story after story emerged during and after the war; the man lived for God and talked directly with God. Whether walking in the forest alone, praying to Heaven, or kneeling, he knew his only hope was correspondence with his Creator. Let us emulate such actions, praising the Lord and seeking Him in all life's affairs.

Throughout this research, one of the essential objectives was to evaluate the Christian worldview, teachings, and beliefs of Stonewall Jackson compared to the orthodox Presbyterian traditional views, including the Westminster Standards and positions held by prominent Presbyterians of his day. Jackson passed the test. Not only did he resemble a confessional Presbyterian, he also clearly maintained the reputation of a Christian man who adhered to *sola Scriptura,* "or Scripture alone." Like the great Reformer John Knox, Jackson evidently carried a Bible in one hand and weaponry in the other. Jackson was no fanatic; he was a Bible-believing Christian who viewed the Scriptures as nothing less than the divine inspiration of the living God. This, too, should challenge us today to revere and submit to God's Holy Word. If one claims the Lord is not with His people today or absent from this fallen world, they have not read the Bible and placed their faith in Christ. The uniqueness of this study centered on the theological positions and teachings of Jackson in the context of his church, the Presbyterian faith. It is the prayer of the author that the reader has gained additional insight into Reformed theology and acknowledges that the doctrine centers on the sovereignty, grace, and love of God. In short, it is God's will that matters and not ours.

As we conclude this study, Stonewall Jackson's life and legacy—and even the man himself—are under attack. Often forgotten and especially important with the recent attacks on members of the Confederate Army, most leaders in the Confederacy at one point served the nation of the United States. Surely, political differences and later regional separation existed to entail a departure from the only country they knew. However, Stonewall and others shed blood, and some even lost their lives, fighting for and defending the United States. Critics often ignore this in today's discussion. Granted, one side of history comprises the victors in the war promoting the Confederate States of America as rebels or enemies of the state. Were any of these men loyal Americans serving their homeland, their father's homeland, and the region from which they originated? The reader must remember that the US Civil War was a combat altercation of brothers fighting brothers, very similar to that of the colonists departing from English rule, often referred to as the first Civil War. In fact, several soldiers from both sides were a generation or two away from fathers and grandfathers who fought in the War of Independence, or the War of 1812. It is crucial, then, to conclude that a considerable number of Southern soldiers honorably served their nation before the war broke out. Jackson's time at VMI was nothing less than a service to this great nation, one we must admire and respect.

The writer did not seek to convince nor instill any direct opinion on the creation of the Confederate States of America. However, the idea remains that unfair attacks often destroy any member's legacy, including professing Christians affiliated with the Confederacy. This study primarily sought to study the Christian faith, involvement, growth, and legacy of Stonewall Jackson. It is irresponsible to profess that genuine believers in Christ did not fight on both sides of the War Between the States. The body of Christ is not a region; it comprises sons and daughters from every land on Earth, also known as the true invisible church of Jesus Christ, commonly referred to in the Reformed tradition as the catholic church (professing Christians).

Objectors removed Jackson's statue, and academia is seeking to erase his legacy. First, we beg to proclaim that Jackson does not care about a standing statue; he might have even disapproved of it. Man should never glorify man but honor the Lord Jesus Christ. Stonewall Jackson is a Christian role model—one we must hold in our hearts and study. The Lord did an amazing work by turning this man into a faithful servant. Who today is without controversy? Jackson was human like you and me. He had his faults and sin and served on the losing side of the Civil War. Today, opponents attack the Confederates as adherents to slavery and nothing else. This is untrue, and it is the prayer of this author that this study brings the realization that Christians served on both sides of the conflict. Jackson felt he was justified in defending his home state under invasion. I urge the reader to consider that you, too, would most likely fight for the state where you reside or the one to which you are connected through a long history.

The legacy of Stonewall Jackson should not be controversial at all. The standards of the Christian are not of this world but of the Lord Jesus Christ. The lessons are many. We should never glorify men but find our assurance and salvation in Jesus Christ. But we

Conclusion

have the right and obligation to study history and respect the hand of the Lord in salvation in the testimonies of other believers. Studying Stonewall Jackson and the Civil War only affirms the Christian position. The world we live in remains fallen, covered in darkness, and in deep need of Jesus Christ.

Thankfully, not everyone has attacked Jackson's legacy and life. You might have had respect and admiration for the general before reading this book. If you did not, it is hopeful that you gained additional insight and honor for Jackson. His legacy indeed continues and survives throughout the globe. Military leaders of the world continue to study his campaigns with awe. May the reader always remember Jackson first as a faithful servant to his Lord Jesus Christ.

Our day is coming, too. Whether we die a sudden death or experience a longer life than Stonewall Jackson, death is a reality that is defeated only by the Lord Jesus Christ. Admire, appreciate, and emulate the faithfulness of Stonewall Jackson. If you seek understanding and freedom from sin, pain, and suffering, follow Christ.

May the Lord allow us to be more like Stonewall Jackson, serving Jesus in every aspect of life. May we acknowledge our weaknesses and sins and call upon the Lord to redeem and sanctify us, and to set us apart from this fallen world. Praise and glory be to Jesus Christ that He saves souls like us and, yes, souls like Stonewall Jackson.

Amen.

Afterword

Slavery

IN OUR CURRENT DAYS, it seems only slavery is associated with the Confederate States of America. Sadly, this is untrue, but this mindset seems to be growing increasingly popular. Stonewall Jackson did own slaves. He obviously did, as indicated by his wife. The believer today should neither find comfort in nor openly embrace such a practice. The Bible does, in fact, reference slavery and acknowledge its existence in both the Old and New Testaments. However, the slavery practiced in the 1800s as a result of the African slave trade appears to depart dramatically from any fair treatment of slaves, regularly referenced in the New Testament (Col. 4:1, Eph. 6:5–9). We must note, the northern states practiced slavery just as the Southern inhabitants did.

From the beginning of the young nation, a peculiar connection to slavery was maintained; it was one that troubled prominent Founders of the government, including Patrick Henry and Thomas Jefferson. All parts of the United States played a role in slavery. Though, sadly only the Confederates seem today to be tainted with the institutions legacy.

Paul spoke of slavery, even saying, "Slaves obey your masters" (Ephesians 6:5). Pro-slavery Christians took such verses and argued that the practice, ordained by God, was entirely justified. From Israel being enslaved themselves to being commanded on how to treat slaves, the Scriptures mentioned the standard. However, any student of history must study and acknowledge that the African Slave Trade, leading up to the institution of slavery practiced in the United States, differed sharply from references to slavery made by the Lord Himself. While no enslaver was the same, a harsh, cruel, almost never-ending institution remained. While we can gather that Stonewall was fair in his treatment, limited accounts remain.

We know today that Jackson personally educated slaves and freed blacks. The fact that he founded an African Sabbath School with his funds and sought to educate free and enslaved African Americans gives credence to the fact that he believed the race was part of God's Kingdom. In fact, Anna made such remarks, sharing that Jackson viewed slaves as children of God.

Christians long played a role in abolishing slavery. Slavery remained a divisive issue: President Lincoln later remarked that both sides read the same Bible but came out with differing interpretations. Perhaps this is precisely where Jackson landed within this debate. A telling argument is that God's will endures in all aspects of life; this logic proves that the Lord desired the abolishment of slavery in the United States. Today the covenant of grace focuses on the life, death, and resurrection of Christ, which further supports a radical change in the behavior of slavery. Jesus died for His people, enabling them to be made new (John 3:6, Titus 3:5).

The Scriptures forbid any physical or sexual assault of any person, including an enslaved person (Rom. 1:29, Matt. 15:19, Eph. 4:32). Second, the Lord's life and ministry on earth enabled a new freedom that humanity had not yet experienced. Christians recollect a theme of "freedom and liberty" connected to the New Testament, a message delivered during the Great Awakening and later in the American Revolution. This same idea existed in abolishing slavery, relying on such a verse: "There is neither Jew nor Greek, there is neither bond nor free, there is neither male nor female: for ye are all one in Christ Jesus" (Gal. 3:28).

Most importantly, the Christian must review the first and greatest commandment: "Master, which is the great commandment in the law? Jesus said unto him, Thou shalt love the Lord thy God with all thy heart, and with all thy soul, and with all thy mind. This is the first and great commandment. And the second is like unto it, Thou shalt love thy neighbour as thyself. On these two commandments hang all the law and the prophets" (Matt. 22:36–40). Abolitionists at the time focused on "loving your neighbor." Lastly, the abolishment of slavery remained inevitable. Whether it was the generation of the 19th century or a generation after, they could not ignore the issue in a growing society that was constantly evolving.

In no way will the writer defend the slavery connected to the United States. However, again using the Providential thought of an omnipresent and omnipotent Creator that Stonewall embraced, God's will on the institution of slavery would be carried out.

Jackson was no controversial figure. Certainly, he was a man of his era and caught up in the debate over slavery. He was on the losing side of the issue, with God's providential hand ending the practice in the United States. We should never remember Jackson as a promoter of slavery, as he was not. He fought for his family and home, like countless other Southerners.

It is the prayer that Jackson be remembered as a faithful Christian, and one who served his fellow man.

Endnotes

Preface

1. George Truett, "The Grace of Patience" (sermon, First Baptist Church of Dallas, Dallas, TX, November 29, 1942), http://digitalcollections.baylor.edu/cdm/search/collection/fa-gwt (accessed February 22, 2017).
2. Westminster Assembly, The Shorter Catechism, (Greenville: Christian Education Ministries, 2020)...A #1.

Chapter 1

3. Byron Farwell, *A Biography of General Thomas J. Jackson*, (New York: W. W. Norton & Company, 1992), 4.
4. Farwell, *A Biography of General Thomas J. Jackson*, 5.
5. Robert Lewis Dabney, *Life and Campaigns of Stonewall Jackson*, (New York: Blelock & Co., 1866), 6.
6. Dabney, *Life and Campaigns of Stonewall Jackson*, 6.
7. Thomas Jackson Arnold, *Early Life and Letters of General Thomas J. Jackson*, (New York: Fleming H. Revell Company, 1916), 25.
8. Arnold, *Early Life and Letters of General Thomas J. Jackson*, 25.
9. Dabney, *Life and Campaigns of Stonewall Jackson*, 6.
10. Ibid., 6.
11. Ibid.
12. Mary Anna Jackson, *Life and Letters of General Thomas J. Jackson*, (1892; reprint, New York: Harper & Brothers, 2019), 21.
13. Farwell, *A Biography of General Thomas J. Jackson*, 5.
14. Roy Bird Cook, *The Family and Early Life of Stonewall Jackson*, (Charleston: Charleston Printing Company, 1948), 5.
15. Cook, *The Family and Early Life of Stonewall Jackson*, 6.
16. Farwell, *A Biography of General Thomas J. Jackson*, 6.
17. Ibid.

18 *Ibid.*
19 *Ibid.*
20 James I. Robertson, Jr., *Stonewall Jackson: The Man, the Soldier, the Legend*, (New York: Macmillan, 1997), 9.
21 Jackson, *Life and Letters of General Thomas J. Jackson*, 19.
22 *Ibid.*, 20.
23 Robert Lewis Dabney, *Life and Campaigns of Stonewall Jackson*, 7.
24 *Ibid.*
25 Arnold, *Early Life and Letters of General Thomas J. Jackson*, 28.
26 Jackson, *Life and Letters of General Thomas J. Jackson*, 22.
27 Lochlainn Seabrook, *The Quotable Stonewall Jackson: Selections from the Writings and Speeches of the South's Most Famous General*, (Franklin: Sea Raven Press, 2012), 27.
28 Farwell, *A Biography of General Thomas J. Jackson*, 8.
29 Jackson, *Life and Letters of General Thomas J. Jackson*, 23.
30 *Ibid.*
31 Dabney, *Life and Campaigns of Stonewall Jackson*, 12.
32 Cook, *The Family and Early Life of Stonewall Jackson*, 37.
33 *Ibid.*
34 Jackson, *Life and Letters of General Thomas J. Jackson*, 26.
35 *Ibid.*
36 *Ibid.*
37 *Ibid.*, 25.
38 Westminster Assembly, *The Westminster Confession of Faith*, (Greenville: Christian Education Ministries, 2014), 45.
39 Dabney, *Life and Campaigns of Stonewall Jackson*, 15.
40 *Ibid.*
41 Robertson Jr., *Stonewall Jackson: The Man, the Soldier, the Legend*, 13.
42 J. Steven Wilkins, *All Things for Good: The Steadfast Fidelity of Stonewall Jackson*, (Nashville: Cumberland House, 2004), 11.
43 Westminster Assembly, *The Shorter Catechism...A* #19.
44 Robert Alexander Webb, *The Reformed Doctrine of Adoption*, (1947; reprint, Harrisonburg: Sprinkle Publications, 2012), 80.

45 Cook, *The Family and Early Life of Stonewall Jackson*, 50.
46 Westminster Assembly, *The Westminster Confession of Faith*, 16.
47 Dabney, *Life and Campaigns of Stonewall Jackson*, 16.
48 *Ibid.*, 15.
49 *Ibid.*, 16.
50 *Ibid.*
51 John R. Richardson, *The Christian Character of General Stonewall Jackson*, (Weaverville: The Southern Presbyterian Journal Company, 1943), 4.
52 *Westminster Assembly (1643-1652). The Westminster Confession*, 21.
53 Cook, *The Family and Early Life of Stonewall Jackson*, 62.
54 Robertson, Jr., *Stonewall Jackson: The Man, the Soldier, the Legend*, 19.
55 Arnold, *Early Life and Letters of General Thomas J. Jackson*, 50.
56 *Ibid.*
57 Cook, *The Family and Early Life of Stonewall Jackson*, 56.
58 *Ibid.*
59 Farwell, *A Biography of General Thomas J. Jackson*, 14.
60 Wilkins, *All Things for Good: The Steadfast Fidelity of Stonewall Jackson*, 15.

CHAPTER 2

61 Jackson, *Life and Letters of General Thomas J. Jackson*, 29.
62 Robertson, Jr., *Stonewall Jackson: The Man, the Soldier, the Legend*, 34.
63 *Ibid.*
64 Jackson, *Life and Letters of General Thomas J. Jackson*, 29.
65 Seabrook, The Quotable Stonewall Jackson: Selections From the Writings and Speeches of the South's Most Famous General, 29.
66 Jackson, *Life and Letters of General Thomas J. Jackson*, 31.
67 Robert Lewis Dabney, *Life and Campaigns of Stonewall Jackson*, 21.
68 Jackson, *Life and Letters of General Thomas J. Jackson*, 32.
69 *Ibid.*
70 Dabney, *Life and Campaigns of Stonewall Jackson*, 23.
71 *Ibid.*

72 *Ibid.*, 24.
73 Jackson, *Life and Letters of General Thomas J. Jackson*, 33.
74 *Ibid.*, 34.
75 Thomas J. Jackson, "Letter fragment. Stonewall Jackson to his sister Laura. April 23, 1846" https://digitalcollections.vmi.edu/digital/collection/p15821coll4/id/37/rec/5 (accessed December 15, 2022).
76 Jackson, *Life and Letters of General Thomas J. Jackson*, 35.
77 *Ibid.*
78 Robertson Jr., *Stonewall Jackson: The Man, the Soldier, the Legend*, 54.
79 *Ibid.*
80 Richardson, *The Christian Character of General Stonewall Jackson*, 7.
81 Robertson Jr., *Stonewall Jackson: The Man, the Soldier, the Legend*, 57.
82 *Ibid.*
83 *Ibid.*
84 Dabney, *Life and Campaigns of Stonewall Jackson*, 33.
85 John Esten Cooke, *Stonewall Jackson: A Military Biography*, (New York: D. Appleton and Company, 1876), 17.
86 Robertson Jr., *Stonewall Jackson: The Man, the Soldier, the Legend*, 51.
87 Arnold, *Early Life and Letters of General Thomas J. Jackson*, 91.
88 William S. Plumer, *Jehovah: A Treatise on Providence*, (1865; reprint, Harrisonburg: Sprinkle Publications, 1997), 21.
89 *Ibid.*
90 Westminster Assembly, *The Westminster Confession of Faith*, 22.
91 John Esten Cooke, *The Life of Stonewall Jackson: From Official Papers, Contemporary Narratives, and Personal Acquaintance*, (1863; reprint, New York: Harper, 2018), 12.
92 *Ibid.*
93 Dabney, *Life and Campaigns of Stonewall Jackson*, 34.
94 *Ibid.*, 35.
95 Westminster Assembly, *The Westminster Confession of Faith*, 25-26.
96 Dabney, *Life and Campaigns of Stonewall Jackson*, 35.
97 Westminster Assembly, *The Shorter Catechism...A* #31.
98 Jackson, *Life and Letters of General Thomas J. Jackson*, 40.

ENDNOTES

99 Richardson, *The Christian Character of General Stonewall Jackson*, 11.
100 Dabney, *Life and Campaigns of Stonewall Jackson*, 35.
101 Ibid., 36.
102 Jackson, *Life and Letters of General Thomas J. Jackson*, 40.
103 Westminster Assembly, *The Shorter Catechism...A #3*.
104 John Esten Cooke, *The Life of Stonewall Jackson: From Official Papers, Contemporary Narratives, and Personal Acquaintance*, 12.
105 Westminster Assembly, *The Westminster Confession of Faith*, 42.
106 Jackson, *Life and Letters of General Thomas J. Jackson*, 40.
107 Ibid.
108 Ibid.
109 Ibid., 41.
110 Ibid.
111 Dabney, *Life and Campaigns of Stonewall Jackson*, 38.
112 Thomas J. Jackson, "Letter. Stonewall Jackson to Uncle (James Jackson), April 24, 1850", https://digitalcollections.vmi.edu/digital/collection/p15821coll4/id/113/rec/19 (accessed December 15, 2022).
113 Thomas J. Jackson, "Letter. Stonewall Jackson to his sister Laura. July 7, 1850", https://digitalcollections.vmi.edu/digital/collection/p15821coll4/id/121/rec/22 (accessed December 15, 2022).
114 Thomas J. Jackson, "Letter. Stonewall Jackson to his sister Laura. April 22, 1851", https://digitalcollections.vmi.edu/digital/collection/p15821coll4/id/136/rec/27 (accessed December 15, 2022).

CHAPTER 3

115 Jackson, *Life and Letters of General Thomas J. Jackson*, 43.
116 Cooke, *Stonewall Jackson: A Military Biography*, 18.
117 Farwell, *A Biography of General Thomas J. Jackson*, 94.
118 Jackson, *Life and Letters of General Thomas J. Jackson*, 45.
119 Cook, *The Family and Early Life of Stonewall Jackson*, 128.
120 Jackson, *Life and Letters of General Thomas J. Jackson*, 46.
121 Ibid.
122 Lewis Dabney, *Life and Campaigns of Stonewall Jackson*, 53.
123 Westminster Assembly, *The Westminster Confession of Faith*, 27.

124 *Ibid.*
125 Cook, *The Family and Early Life of Stonewall Jackson*, 129.
126 *Westminster Assembly (1643-1652). The Westminster Confession.*
127 *Ibid.*
128 Charles Hodge, *Systematic Theology*, (1992; reprint Phillipsburg: P&R Publishing, 1988), 87.
129 Robert Lewis Dabney, *The Five Points of Calvinism*, (1895; reprint Harrisonburg: Sprinkle Publications, 1992), 41.
130 Westminster Assembly, *The Westminster Confession of Faith*, 33.
131 Robert Lewis Dabney, *Life and Campaigns of Stonewall Jackson*, 54.
132 Cooke, *Stonewall Jackson: A Military Biography*, 19.
133 Westminster Assembly, *The Shorter Catechism…A* #35.
134 Farwell, *A Biography of General Thomas J. Jackson*, 96.
135 Cooke, *Stonewall Jackson: A Military Biography*, 23.
136 *Ibid.*
137 *Ibid.*, 25.
138 William S. Plumer, *Theology for the People or Biblical Doctrine, Plainly Stated*, (1875; reprint, Harrisonburg: Sprinkle Publications, 2005), 163.
139 Hodge, *Systematic Theology*, 498.
140 Arnold, *Early Life and Letters of General Thomas J. Jackson*, 181.
141 Westminster Assembly, *The Westminster Confession of Faith*, 13.
142 Jackson, *Life and Letters of General Thomas J. Jackson*, 49.
143 Thomas J. Jackson, "Letter. Stonewall Jackson to his sister Laura. April 1, 1853," https://digitalcollections.vmi.edu/digital/collection/p15821coll4/id/204/rec/21 (accessed January 2023).
144 Thomas J. Jackson, "Letter. Stonewall Jackson to his sister Laura. June 6, 1853," https://digitalcollections.vmi.edu/digital/collection/p15821coll4/id/213/rec/23 (accessed January 2023).
145 Westminster Assembly, *The Westminster Confession of Faith*, 41.
146 Arnold, *Early Life and Letters of General Thomas J. Jackson*, 195.
147 Jackson, *Life and Letters of General Thomas J. Jackson*, 49.
148 *Ibid.*
149 Cooke, *Stonewall Jackson: A Military Biography*, 20.
150 Lewis Dabney, *Life and Campaigns of Stonewall Jackson*, 44.

151 *Ibid.*

152 *Ibid.*

153 Robertson Jr., *Stonewall Jackson: The Man, the Soldier, the Legend*, 119.

154 Thomas J. Jackson, "Letter. Stonewall Jackson to his sister Laura. April 7, 1854," https://digitalcollections.vmi.edu/digital/collection/p15821coll4/id/241/rec/30 (accessed January 2023).

155 Thomas J. Jackson, "Letter. Stonewall Jackson to his Aunt. May 19, 1856," https://digitalcollections.vmi.edu/digital/collection/p15821coll4/id/346/rec/56 (accessed January 2023).

156 Westminster Assembly, *The Shorter Catechism…A* #99.

157 Jackson, *Life and Letters of General Thomas J. Jackson*, 47.

158 *Ibid.*, 54.

159 *Ibid.*

160 Cooke, *Stonewall Jackson: A Military Biography*, 21.

161 *Ibid.*

162 *Ibid.*, 22.

163 *Ibid.*, 30.

164 *Ibid.*

165 Westminster Assembly, *The Shorter Catechism…A* #11.

166 Hodge, *Systematic Theology*, 222.

167 *Ibid.*

168 *Ibid.*

169 Farwell, *A Biography of General Thomas J. Jackson*, 124.

170 Jackson, *Life and Letters of General Thomas J. Jackson*, 47.

171 Thomas J. Jackson, "Letter. Stonewall Jackson to John Lyle Campbell. June 7, 1858", https://digitalcollections.vmi.edu/digital/collection/p15821coll4/id/433/rec/75 (accessed January 2023).

172 Richardson, *The Christian Character of General Stonewall Jackson*, 14.

173 Farwell, *A Biography of General Thomas J. Jackson*, 125.

174 *Ibid.*

175 Jackson, *Life and Letters of General Thomas J. Jackson*, 58.

176 Thomas J. Jackson, "Letter. Stonewall Jackson to his sister Laura. February 8, 1858", https://digitalcollections.vmi.edu/digital/collection/p15821coll4/id/413/rec/70 (accessed January 2023).

177 Charles Hodge, *Systematic Theology*, (Phillipsburg: P&R Publishing, 1988), 459.
178 Westminster Assembly, *The Westminster Confession of Faith*, 43.
179 Wilkins, *All Things for Good: The Steadfast Fidelity of Stonewall Jackson*, 74.
180 Robertson Jr., *Stonewall Jackson: The Man, the Soldier, the Legend*, 125.
181 Ibid.

Chapter 4

182 Jackson, *Life and Letters of General Thomas J. Jackson*, 62.
183 Robertson Jr., *Stonewall Jackson: The Man, the Soldier, the Legend*, 144.
184 William S. Plumer, Theo*logy for the People or Biblical Doctrine, Plainly Stated*, 153.
185 Arnold, *Early Life and Letters of General Thomas J. Jackson*, 204.
186 Robertson Jr., *Stonewall Jackson: The Man, the Soldier, the Legend*, 144.
187 Byron Farwell, *A Biography of General Thomas J. Jackson*, 114.
188 Ibid.
189 Westminster Assembly, *The Shorter Catechism…A* #60.
190 Westminster Assembly, *The Westminster Confession of Faith*, 56.
191 Ibid., 50.
192 William S. Plumer, *Theology for the People or Biblical Doctrine, Plainly Stated*, 164.
193 Westminster Assembly, *The Shorter Catechism…A* #39, 40.
194 Westminster Assembly, *The Westminster Confession of Faith*, 50.
195 Farwell, *A Biography of General Thomas J. Jackson*, 114.
196 Arnold, *Early Life and Letters of General Thomas J. Jackson*, 204.
197 Ibid., 208.
198 Ibid., 209.
199 Plumer, *Theology for the People or Biblical Doctrine, Plainly Stated*, 195.
200 Ibid., 198.
201 Farwell, *A Biography of General Thomas J. Jackson*, 115.
202 Charles Hodge, *Systematic Theology*, 499.

203 G.F.R. Henderson, *Stonewall Jackson and the American Civil War*, (1943; reprint, New York: Da Capo Press Inc., 1988), 124.

204 Westminster Assembly, *The Westminster Confession of Faith*, 15.

205 Henderson, *Stonewall Jackson and the American Civil War*, 124.

206 Benjamin Morgan Palmer, *Select Writings of Benjamin Morgan Palmer*, (1892; reprint, Edinburgh: Banner of Truth Trust, 2014), 35

207 Jackson, *Life and Letters of General Thomas J. Jackson*, 62.

208 Robert Lewis Dabney, *Life and Campaigns of Stonewall Jackson*, 72.

209 *Ibid.*

210 Jackson, *Life and Letters of General Thomas J. Jackson*, 63.

211 *Ibid.*, 63.

212 Farwell, *A Biography of General Thomas J. Jackson*, 117.

213 Dabney, *Life and Campaigns of Stonewall Jackson*, 73.

214 Arnold, *Early Life and Letters of General Thomas J. Jackson*, 247.

215 Jackson, *Life and Letters of General Thomas J. Jackson*, 65.

216 Dabney, *Life and Campaigns of Stonewall Jackson*, 73.

217 Jackson, *Life and Letters of General Thomas J. Jackson*, 69.

218 Arnold, *Early Life and Letters of General Thomas J. Jackson*, 255.

219 Jackson, *Life and Letters of General Thomas J. Jackson*, 66.

220 *Ibid.*

221 Westminster Assembly, *The Westminster Confession of Faith*, 61.

222 Jackson, *Life and Letters of General Thomas J. Jackson*, 73.

223 Farwell, *A Biography of General Thomas J. Jackson*, 130.

224 Jackson, *Life and Letters of General Thomas J. Jackson*, 75.

225 Westminster Assembly, *The Shorter Catechism...A* #2, 3.

226 Dabney, *Life and Campaigns of Stonewall Jackson*, 75.

227 Jackson, *Life and Letters of General Thomas J. Jackson*, 77.

228 *Ibid.*, 80.

229 *Ibid.*, 81.

230 *Ibid.*, 82.

231 *Ibid.*, 83.

232 *Ibid.*

233 Richard G. Williams Jr., *Stonewall Jackson: The Black Man's Best Friend*, (Nashville: Cumberland House Publishing Inc., 2006), 74.

234 Arnold, *Early Life and Letters of General Thomas J. Jackson*, 259.

235 Ibid., 260.

236 Ibid., 262.

237 Arnold, *Early Life and Letters of General Thomas J. Jackson*, 263.

238 Westminster Assembly, *The Westminster Confession of Faith*, 34.

239 Arnold, *Early Life and Letters of General Thomas J. Jackson*, 276.

240 Jackson, *Life and Letters of General Thomas J. Jackson*, 86.

241 Ibid., 88.

242 Westminster Assembly, *The Westminster Confession of Faith*, 39.

Chapter 5

243 Farwell, *A Biography of General Thomas J. Jackson*, 142.

244 Arnold, *Early Life and Letters of General Thomas J. Jackson*, 291.

245 Cook, *The Family and Early Life of Stonewall Jackson*, 155.

246 Jackson, *Life and Letters of General Thomas J. Jackson*, 95.

247 Ibid., 96.

248 Ibid.

249 Ibid.

250 R.L. Dabney, "The Christian Soldier" (sermon, College Church, VA, December 14, 1862).

251 Ibid.

252 George C. Rable, *God's Almost Chosen Peoples: A Religious History of the American Civil War* (Chapel Hill: The University of North Carolina Press, 2010), 38.

253 Ibid., 38.

254 Westminster Assembly, *The Westminster Confession of Faith*, 22.

255 Charles Hodge, *Systematic Theology*, 216.

256 Jackson, *Life and Letters of General Thomas J. Jackson*, 97.

257 Arnold, *Early Life and Letters of General Thomas J. Jackson*, 294.

258 Cooke, *Stonewall Jackson: A Military Biography*, 34.

259 Arnold, *Early Life and Letters of General Thomas J. Jackson*, 296.

260 Cooke, *Stonewall Jackson: A Military Biography*, 35.
261 *Ibid.*
262 Jackson, *Life and Letters of General Thomas J. Jackson*, 103.
263 *Ibid.*, 105.
264 Cooke, *Stonewall Jackson: A Military Biography*, 41.
265 Jackson, *Life and Letters of General Thomas J. Jackson*, 107.
266 *Ibid.*, 108.
267 *Ibid.*, 109.
268 *Ibid.*, 110.
269 *Ibid.*
270 Cook, *The Family and Early Life of Stonewall Jackson*, 160.
271 Cooke, *Stonewall Jackson: A Military Biography*, 67.
272 *Ibid.*, 72.
273 *Ibid.*, 73.
274 Charles Hodge, *Systematic Theology*, 459.
275 *Ibid.*, 220.
276 Westminster Assembly, *The Westminster Confession of Faith*, 23.
277 Jackson, *Life and Letters of General Thomas J. Jackson*, 118.
278 *Ibid.*, 120.
279 Cook, *The Family and Early Life of Stonewall Jackson*, 161.
280 Richardson, *The Christian Character of General Stonewall Jackson*, 16.
281 William S. Plumer, *Theology for the People or Biblical Doctrine, Plainly Stated*, 139.
282 Westminster Assembly, *The Westminster Confession of Faith*, 43.
283 Jackson, *Life and Letters of General Thomas J. Jackson*, 122.
284 *Ibid.*, 128.
285 James I. Robertson Jr., *The Stonewall Brigade*, (Baton Rouge: Louisiana State Press, 1963), 46.
286 *Ibid.*, 47.
287 James I. Robertson Jr., *The Stonewall Brigade*, 88.
288 Jackson, *Life and Letters of General Thomas J. Jackson*, 134.
289 Robertson Jr., *The Stonewall Brigade*, 25.

290 Richardson, *The Christian Character of General Stonewall Jackson*, 20.

291 Cooke, *The Life of Stonewall Jackson: From Official Papers, Contemporary Narratives, and Personal Acquaintance*, 27.

292 William S. Plumer, *Assurance of Grace and Salvation: What It Is; How To Attain It; Why More Do Not Enjoy It*, (Harrisonburg: Sprinkle Publications, 1997), 143.

293 Westminster Assembly, *The Westminster Confession of Faith*, 39.

294 W.W. Bennett, *The Great Revival in the Southern Armies*, (1877; reprint, Harrisonburg: Sprinkle Publications, 1989), 140.

295 Jackson, *Life and Letters of General Thomas J. Jackson*, 135.

296 *Ibid.*, 136.

297 *Ibid.*

CHAPTER 6

298 Jackson, *Life and Letters of General Thomas J. Jackson*, 162.

299 *Ibid.*

300 Robert Lewis Dabney, *Life and Campaigns of Stonewall Jackson*, (1866; reprint, Harrisonburg: Sprinkle Publications, 1983), 329.

301 Jackson, *Life and Letters of General Thomas J. Jackson*, 162.

302 Plumer, *The Bible True, and Infidelity Wicked*, (1880; reprint, Harrisonburg: Sprinkle Publications, 2000), 237.

303 Westminster Assembly, *The Westminster Confession of Faith*, 48.

304 Jackson, *Life and Letters of General Thomas J. Jackson*, 238.

305 William S. Plumer, *The Christian*, (Harrisonburg: Sprinkle Publications, 1997), 85.

306 Dabney, *Life and Campaigns of Stonewall Jackson*, 330.

307 *Ibid.*, 168.

308 Cooke, *Stonewall Jackson: A Military Biography*, 102.

309 Rable, *God's Almost Chosen Peoples: A Religious History of the American Civil War*, 138.

310 James Henley Thornwell, *The Collected Writings of James Henley Thornwell: Volume 3*, (Edinburgh: The Banner of Truth Trust, 1986), 94.

311 Westminster Assembly, *The Shorter Catechism...A* #7.

312 J. Williams Jones, *Christ in the Camp: Or, Religion in the Confederate Army*, (Atlanta: The Martin & Hoyt Co., 1904), 93.

313 Dabney, *Life and Campaigns of Stonewall Jackson*, 413.

314 Charles Hodge, *Systematic Theology*, 505.

315 Jackson, *Life and Letters of General Thomas J. Jackson*, 185.

316 Cooke, *Stonewall Jackson: A Military Biography*, 198.

317 Richardson, *The Christian Character of General Stonewall Jackson*, 19.

318 W.B. Sprague, *Letters to Young Men*, (Harrisonburg: Sprinkle Publications, 1988), 189.

319 *Ibid.*, 191.

320 Jedediah Hotchkiss, *Make Me a Map of the Valley: The Civil War Journal of Stonewall Jackson's Topographer*, (Dallas: Southern Methodist University Press, 1973), 57.

321 Henderson, *Stonewall Jackson and the American Civil War*, 369.

322 Jackson, *Life and Letters of General Thomas J. Jackson*, 194.

323 *Ibid.*

324 *Ibid.*, 202.

325 *Ibid.*, 210.

326 *Ibid.*

327 *Ibid.*, 211.

328 *Ibid.*

329 Jones, *Christ in the Camp: Or, Religion in the Confederate Army*, 92.

330 Westminster Assembly, *The Shorter Catechism...A* #1.

331 Dabney, *Life and Campaigns of Stonewall Jackson*, 507.

332 *Ibid.*, 537.

333 Henry Kyd Douglas, *I Rode with Stonewall*, (Greenwich: Premier Civil War Classics, 1961), 143.

334 *Ibid.*

335 Jackson, *Life and Letters of General Thomas J. Jackson*, 233.

336 *Ibid.*, 234.

337 *Ibid.*, 242.

338 *Ibid.*

339 *Ibid.*, 243.

340 Ibid., 256.
341 Archibald Alexander, *Practical Truths*, (Harrisonburg: Sprinkle Publications, 1998) ,64.
342 Dabney, *Life and Campaigns of Stonewall Jackson*, 588.
343 Westminster Assembly, *The Westminster Confession of Faith*, 40.
344 Dabney, *Life and Campaigns of Stonewall Jackson*, 643.
345 Douglas, *I Rode with Stonewall*, 42.
346 Jones, *Christ in the Camp: Or, Religion in the Confederate Army*, 97.
347 Douglas, *I Rode with Stonewall*, 97.
348 Charles L. Dufour, *Nine Men in Gray*, (Garden City: Doubleday & Company Inc., 1963), 14.
349 Ibid.
350 Jackson, *Life and Letters of General Thomas J. Jackson*, 257.
351 Westminster Assembly, *The Westminster Confession of Faith*, 13.
352 Ibid., 63.
353 Arnold, *Early Life and Letters of General Thomas J. Jackson*, 344.
354 Henry Alexander White, *Southern Presbyterian Leaders 1683–1911*, (Edinburgh: The Banner of Truth, 2000), 448.
355 Richardson, *The Christian Character of General Stonewall Jackson*, 3.
356 Dabney, *Life and Campaigns of Stonewall Jackson*, 384.
357 Douglas, *I Rode with Stonewall*, 77.
358 Dabney, *Life and Campaigns of Stonewall Jackson*, 641.
359 Ibid., 644.
360 William S. Plumer, *Jehovah-Jireh: A Treatise on Providence*, 163.
361 Ibid., 209.
362 Dabney, *Life and Campaigns of Stonewall Jackson*, 649.
363 Confederate States of America, *Prayers Suitable for the Times in Which We Live*, (Charleston: Evans & Cogswell, 1861), 3.
364 Douglas, *I Rode with Stonewall*, 193.
365 Jones, *Christ in the Camp: Or, Religion in the Confederate Army*, 96.
366 Cooke, *Stonewall Jackson: A Military Biography*, 418.
367 Ibid., 419.
368 Arnold, *Early Life and Letters of General Thomas J. Jackson*, 346.

369 *Ibid.*

370 *Ibid.*

371 Jackson, *Life and Letters of General Thomas J. Jackson*, 290.

372 *Ibid.*, 293.

373 *Ibid.*, 295.

374 Jones, *Christ in the Camp: Or, Religion in the Confederate Army*, 98.

375 *Ibid.*, 100.

376 Jackson, *Life and Letters of General Thomas J. Jackson*, 301.

377 *Ibid.*

378 *Ibid.*, 302.

379 Jones, *Christ in the Camp: Or, Religion in the Confederate Army*, 101.

380 William S. Plumer, *Theology for the People or Biblical Doctrine, Plainly Stated*, 198.

381 Westminster Assembly, *The Shorter Catechism…A* #37.

382 Jones, *Christ in the Camp: Or, Religion in the Confederate Army*, 76.

383 *Ibid.*, 88.

384 Richardson, *The Christian Character of General Stonewall Jackson*, 15.

385 Dabney, *Life and Campaigns of Stonewall Jackson*, 740.

386 Cooke, *The Life of Stonewall Jackson: From Official Papers, Contemporary Narratives, and Personal Acquaintance*, 233.

About the Author

DAVID T. CRUM serves as an Assistant Professor of History at a Christian university. David has an undergraduate degree and two M.A. degrees in Theological Studies and History. He also earned a Doctor of Philosophy degree in Historical Theology.

His research interests include the history of warfare and Christianity. He has a particular interest in studying the work of Stonewall Jackson and George W. Truett. David has taught history, philosophy, American government, and Christian studies courses.

His articles have been published by Abbeville Institute, The Aquila Report, Right Side Broadcasting, the Florida Baptist Historical Society, and several academic journals.

Originally from the Southwest (Colorado and Arizona), David and his wife, Ailene, and their children live in the woods of northern Maine.

SOUTHERN BOOKS. NO APOLOGIES

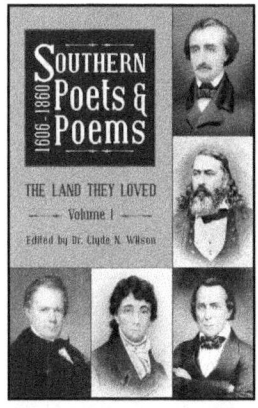

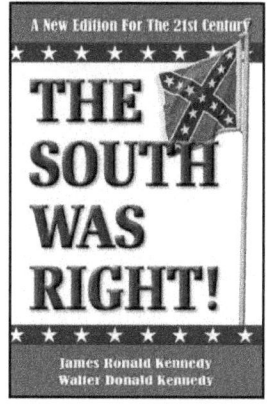

OVER 90 TITLES FOR YOU TO ENJOY

SHOTWELLPUBLISHING.COM

JEFFERY ADDICOTT
Union Terror: Debunking the False Justifications for Union Terror

MARK ATKINS
Women in Combat: Feminism Goes to War

JOYCE BENNETT
Maryland, My Maryland: The Cultural Cleansing of a Small Southern State

GARRY BOWERS
Slavery and The Civil War: What Your History Teacher Didn't Tell You

Dixie Days: Reminiscences Of a Southern Boyhood

JERRY BREWER
Dismantling the Republic

ANDREW P. CALHOUN
My Own Darling Wife: Letters From A Confederate Volunteer

JOHN CHODES
Segregation: Federal Policy or Racism?

Washington's Kkk: The Union League During Southern Reconstruction

WALTER BRIAN CISCO
War Crimes Against Southern Civilians

JOHN DEVANNY
Continuities: The South in a Time of Revolution

JOSHUA DOGGRELL
Doxed: The Political Lynching of a Southern Cop

JAMES C. EDWARDS
What Really Happened?: Quantrill's Raid On Lawrence, Kansas

TED EHMANN
Boom & Bust In Bone Valley: Florida's Phosphate Mining History 1886-2021

JOHN AVERY EMISON
The Deep State Assassination of Martin Luther King Jr.

DON GORDON
Snowball's Chance: My Kidneys Failed, My Wife Left Me & My Dog Died...

JOHN R. GRAHAM
Constitutional History of Secession

PAUL C. GRAHAM
Confederaphobia

When The Yankees Come: Former Carolina Slaves Remember

Nonsense on Stilts: The Gettysburg Address & Lincoln's Imaginary Nation

JOE D. HAINES
The Diary of Col. John Henry Stover Funk of the Stonewall Brigade, 1861-1862

CHARLES HAYES
The REAL First Thanksgiving

V.P. Hughes

Col. John Singleton Mosby: In the News 1862-1916

Terry Hulsey

25 Texas Heroes

The Constitution of Non-State Government:
Field Guide to Texas Secession

Joseph Jay

Sacred Conviction:
The South's Stand for Biblical Authority

Suzanne Johnson

Maxcy Gregg's Sporting Journals 1842-1858

James R. Kennedy

Dixie Rising: Rules For Rebels

Nullifying Federal and State Gun Control:
A How-To Guide For Gun Owners

When Rebel Was Cool:
Growing Up In Dixie, 1950-1965

Walter D. Kennedy

The South's Struggle: America's Hope

Lincoln, The Non-Christian President:
Exposing The Myth

Lincoln, Marx, and the GOP

J.R. & W.D. Kennedy

Jefferson Davis: High Road to Emancipation
and Constitutional Government

Yankee Empire:
Aggressive Abroad and Despotic at Home

Punished With Poverty: The Suffering South

The South Was Right! 3rd Edition

Lewis Liberman

Snowflake Buddies; ABC Leftism For Kids!

Philip Leigh

The Devil's Town: Hot Springs During
The Gangster Era

U.S. Grant's Failed Presidency

The Causes of the Civil War

The Dreadful Frauds: Critical Race Theory
And Identity Politics

Jack Marquardt

Around The World In 80 Years: Confessions
of a Connecticut Confederate

Michael Martin

Southern Grit: Sensing The Siege at Petersburg

Samuel Mitcham

The Greatest Lynching In American History:
New York, 1863

Confederate Patton: Richard Taylor and
The Red River Campaign

Charles T. Pace

Lincoln As He Really Was

Southern Independence. Why War? The War
To Prevent Southern Independence

James R. Roesch

From Founding Fathers To Fire Eaters

Kirkpatrick Sale

Emancipation Hell: The Tragedy Wrought
By Lincoln's Emancipation Proclamation

JOSEPH SCOTCHIE

*The Asheville Connection:
The Making of a Conservative*

ANNE W. SMITH

Charlottesville Untold: Inside Unite The Right

Robert E. Lee: A History for Kids

KAREN STOKES

A Legion Of Devils: Sherman In South Carolina

*The Burning of Columbia, S.C.: A Review
of Northern Assertions and Southern Facts*

*Fortunes of War:
The Adventures of a German Confederate*

*A Confederate in Paris:
Letters of A. Dudley Mann 1867-1879*

JACK TROTTER

Last Train to Dixie

JOHN THEURSAM

Key West's Civil War

H.V. TRAYWICK, JR.

*Along The Shadow Line:
A Road Trip through History and Memory
on the Old Confederate Border*

LESLIE TUCKER

*Old Times There Should Not Be Forgotten:
Cultural Genocide In Dixie*

JOHN VINSON

Southerner Take Your Stand!

MARK R. WINCHELL

*Confessions of a Copperhead:
Culture and Politics in the Modern South*

CLYDE N. WILSON

Calhoun: A Statesman for the 21st Century

*Lies My Teacher Told Me: The True History
of the War For Southern Independence*

The Yankee Problem: An American Dilemma

*Annals Of The Stupid Party:
Republicans Before Trump*

*Nullification:
Reclaiming The Consent of the Governed*

The Old South: 50 Essential Books

The War Between The States: 60 Essential Books

*Reconstruction and the New South, 1865-1913:
50 Essential Books*

*The South 20th Century And Beyond:
50 Essential Books*

*Southern Poets and Poems, 1606-1860:
The Land They Loved, Volume 1*

Looking For Mr. Jefferson

African American Slavery in Historical Perspective

JOE WOLVERTON

*What Degree Of Madness?: Madison's Method
To Make American States Again*

WALTER KIRK WOOD

*Beyond Slavery: The Northern Romantic
Nationalist Origins of America's Civil War*

Green Altar (Literary Imprint)

CATHARINE BROSMAN

An Aesthetic Education and Other Stories (2nd Edition)

Chained Tree, Chained Owls: Poems

Aerosols and Other Poems

RANDALL IVEY

A New England Romance: And Other Southern Stories

JAMES E. KIBBLER, JR.

Tiller : Clayback County Series, Vol. 4

THOMAS MOORE

A Fatal Mercy: The Man Who Lost The Civil War

PERRIN LOVETT

The Substitute, Tom Ironsides 1

KAREN STOKES

Belles

Carolina Love Letters

Carolina Twilight

Honor in the Dust

The Immortals

The Soldier's Ghost: A Tale of Charleston

WILLIAM THOMAS

Runaway Haley: An Imagined Family Saga

Gold-Bug
(Mystery & Suspense Imprint)

BRANDI PERRY

Splintered: A New Orleans Tale

MARTIN WILSON

To Jekyll and Hide

Free Book Offer

DON'T GET LEFT OUT, Y'ALL.
Sign-up and be the first to know about new releases, sales, and other goodies —plus we'll send you TWO FREE EBOOKS!

Lies My Teacher Told Me:
The True History of the War for Southern Independence
by Dr. Clyde N. Wilson

When The Yankees Come
Former Carolina Slaves Remember Sherman's March From the Sea
by Paul C. Graham

FreeLiesBook.com

Southern Books. No Apologies.
We love the South — its history, traditions, and culture — and are proud of our inheritance as Southerners. Our books are a reflection of this love.

www.ingramcontent.com/pod-product-compliance
Lightning Source LLC
Chambersburg PA
CBHW050110170426
43198CB00014B/2522